CHOOSE LOVE

CHOOSE LOVE

the coffee table book that feeds your soul

TRACY McMENIMEN

CHOOSE LOVE: The Coffee Table Book That Feeds Your Soul
Copyright © 2024 Tracy McMenimen

All rights reserved, including the right to reproduce distribute, or transmit in any form or by any means.

Except as permitted under the U.S. Copyright Act of 1976, no part of this book may be reproduced, distributed, or transmitted in any form or by any means, or stored in a database or retrieval system without the written permission of the author, except in the case of brief passages embodied in critical reviews and articles where the title, author and ISBN accompany such review or article.

For information contact: onesister@verizon.net

Published by: Creators Publishing

Cover photo: Tracy McMenimen

Photo credit for title page: istockphoto.com • Marcus Lindstrom

Cover design and interior book design by Francine Platt, Eden Graphics, Inc.

Unless otherwise indicated, Scripture quotations are from the ESV® Bible (The Holy Bible, English Standard Version®), copyright © 2001 by Crossway. Used by permission. All rights reserved.

Hardback ISBN 979-8-9913590-0-9

Manufactured in the United States of America

First Edition

This book is dedicated to those whom I love ...

GOD
my Heavenly Father

You lifted me out of the darkness & gave me new life.
I am grateful for all the miracles, blessings & grace You
have bestowed upon me, but mostly for the LOVE.
— *always, Your beautiful daughter*

LUKE
my son my son

You have loved me "with all the love the world has to give"
...abundantly, effortlessly, constantly... I am a better woman because of you.
— *XOXO, mommadukes*

FAMILY
you & you & you & you

It is your presence, compassion, humor & unconditional love
that always mattered most. I am Me because of You.
— *love, mom's favorite*

GIRLFRIENDS!!!
& a few good men

From the east coast to the midwest & everywhere in between
You light up my life & bring meaning to friendship.
— *♡♡♡, me*

Do everything in love.

1 Corinthians 16:14

While I enjoy my morning coffee, I read something that brings life to my soul. It could be a devotional, The Bible, a be-a-better-me book, *A Course in Miracles* or my latest read-for-fun books. This time alone, all by myself, brings me so much joy.

I'm reminded of how easy it is to choose an old pattern of conversation or choose a new way of expression. Can you see past the judgement you put upon yourself to look at the Truth of your being? Do you have the courage to put down the cozy blanket of complacency and your made-up stories that seem to keep you safe? Would you overlook what your eyes see and be alert with what the heart knows? Would you say no to someone's attention and affection and save your soul?

How about you go through today with less—NO WAIT—how about you go through today with NO self-judgement, NO self-condemnation and NO self-ridicule? What if for today you acknowledge how magnificent you are, how flat out fabulous you are? What if you identify a unique gift you have and then share your brilliance with others? How about that?

AND... While you're at it.... just love?

All there is, is love. ❤

 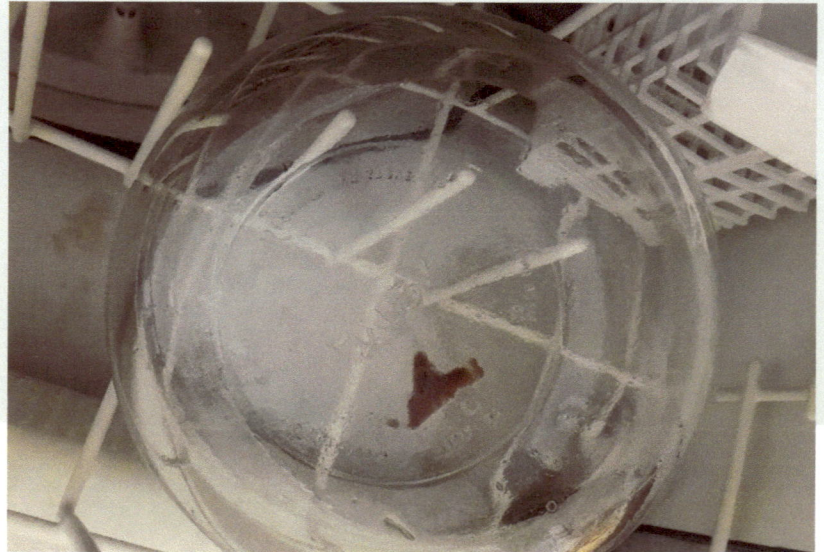

Hush. Walk in the way of love. Boldly. Softly. Fear no evil. No shadow of the night covers you. The veil is lifted. Can you feel it? EVERY. Every. Every scar is healed, every grievance forgiven, every sickness removed. Every accusation erased, every illusion revealed, every condemnation released and yes every perception faded. EVERY.

All that's left is a mist of what was. Gone into the wind. Poof.

Begin today with a kind act, a thoughtful gesture, a smile toward a stranger... JUST BECAUSE. Plant the seed of love and watch it ripple out and out and out. Watch a life change right before your eyes from the effect you caused... JUST BECAUSE.

You. Yes YOU!

The domino effect, the butterfly effect, the snowball effect, the ripple effect, how about the compounding effect....whichever Universal Law you choose... begin today...transform lives... change the world. xoxo

A friend asked me, "With so much hatred in the world do you really believe that everyone has love inside them and deserves love?" My response was, "HECK YAH!" It's this fallen world we live in that alters and influences people. It's all the imperfections, judgements, sinfulness, burdens and illusions… that changes people. The LOVE has always been there. It still is. You just might have to look a little longer.

As a result of all that recklessness and ugliness that lives around us, it creeps into the crevices of our hearts…. we become tainted. Remember the song "Tainted Love" by Soft Cell? Give it a listen. Someone was speaking from that place and wanted to run away, to get away.

AND unfortunately, some people stay broken, some live in chaos, some don't know their worth, some live strangled by the darkness, while others carry generational curses, some have lost their trust in society or have lived through trauma. I could go on and on… etc. etc. etc.

But WE. WE. WE know better. WE are God's children. WE are here to make a difference, WE stand in the gap and WE just LOVE. xoxo

How debilitating are isolation and separation? How depleting are illusions and confusion? Just because we live in a broken world with disarray all around us doesn't mean that we have to act according to those ways.

We can choose to release grievances, to walk away from the lies of the enemy and to be free from the burdens of condemnation, shame and guilt.

We can be the eyes, ears, hands and feet of the One who sent us.

We can be the voice for those in despair, in depression, in overwhelm.

We can be the beacon of His love and light to those who are stuck in the trenches, hiding in the darkness, struggling to just get by.

THAT can be our purpose in the present! We can rise above our mess and be a ray of sunshine to another.

Our purpose may never be a grandiose gesture, an awarded accolade or a moment in the limelight. It could JUST be to reach out to the lost and lonely and BE the LOVE!!!! Again and again and again. xoxo

Have you ever sat in the stillness of the moment with no agenda? No distractions. No plans. No expectations of what should be there.

Have you ever been engulfed with an emptiness that's overshadowed with an abundance of joy? With a simmering soft ebb and flow of nothing? No words. No thoughts to beckon you elsewhere. No discomfort to stay.

Have you ever felt God's presence in your situation as it presses down on your life? With a quiet assurance of full-on peace? No reasons to hide. No anxieties to wear you down. No upsets running rampant.

It is a wonderous feeling to be speechless because life is so good. To have no stories to babble about, no drama to stir up, no feelings of the need to please with guilt at its tail.

I pray that your life grows into a peaceful place, of calmness and certainty, and a journey that is rooted in love. All there is, is LOVE. ❤

"Come out come out, wherever you are. I miss you." – signed "LOVE"

Why are you hiding behind all the busyness, ignoring the problems of yesterday, over-doing things, running your racket, rushing quickly to what's next, ignoring the still small voice inside? Why is this your auto pilot within the gamete of life? What has you on overdrive again?

Stop and think about it. It's automatic because it's what you allow. (Ouch)

If you want the outcome to be different…. grab your imaginary suitcase, fill it with childish laughter, joyous singing, quirky happy-ness, anything else you can think of that pushes you out of the comfort of where you hide into a place of exuberance and silliness and over-flowing fun. Grab your adventurous spirit, your dog-eat-dog spunk and your Captain's Cape and meet me in the field of flowers where the music is blaring, the dancing in merry-go-round circles and playing hero warrior goes on and on and on.

I'll be waiting.

Just LOVE.

 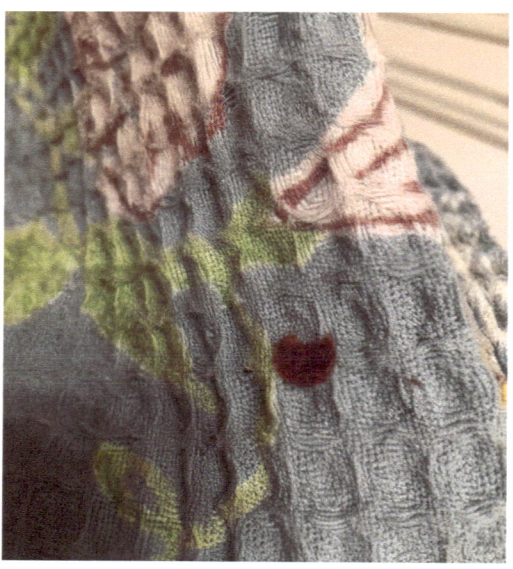 

When you decide to love yourself and change your life for the better, you will have naysayers. Others may feel jealous or envy toward you. You could possibly be ridiculed and challenged. They may yell — "who do you think you are? Loving on yourself? Bragging about yourself? Putting yourself first before us?"

You might also be shunned and ignored. BUT, you cannot let other people's darkness keep you from your light.

You get to decide if you want to share your heart OR hold it tight to the vest. **You** get to choose if you want to step out in truth OR stay coiled up in fear. **You** get to pick what to do in the moment to change the outcome.

Some days you might have to dig a little deeper to find a spark of love to share and other days you're overflowing with so much that you feel like you're walking on air. AND if on any given day you've got nothin' left then maybe that's the day that you reach out to a friend who's shining from the inside out…and ask them to share some of theirs with you.

There's always enough to go around!! xoxo   Just LOVE.

God does not love like the world does. His love is unconditional, never failing, boundless and oftentimes even beyond explanation. IF God is Love. AND God dwells in us. Then it must be true that LOVE dwells in us. It must be true that we are love. Right? Now that's GOOD NEWS!

What? You can't see it? You can't feel it? You don't believe it? Is it because you built up a barrier? A fearful nature? An imaginary brick wall? Or is it that your past is running your love so far into the deepest depths of despair, in the lowest of lowest of places, that you're having a hard time acknowledging that there's any like, never mind love in there anywhere? Is it because someone broke your heart in two and it's empty?

Helloooo Helloooo Helloooooo.... LOVE is in there!!! Keep calling.

SPOILER ALERT... you don't believe in God? Well that doesn't negate the fact that LOVE dwells in you. ....Love lives inside of you and you and you and them and him and her. It Just Does. Go deeper. All there is, is LOVE! ❤

How long? How long are you going to wage war with yourself? How long are you going to deny the forgiveness, salvation and atonement that are yours? How long are you going to listen to the ego's illusions as it sets you up for failure and destruction? How long will you do it alone?

Oh my friend, this is madness. When you fall away or make a mistake, all that is required is a correction. NOT punishment. NOT guilt. NOT shame. NOT suffering. NOT condemnation. NO. The struggle from your hidden agenda, foul attacks on your heart and justifications of wrongdoing are lies to keep you in defeat. Stand tall. Reclaim your Truth.

Rise Up! Rise up from the mud puddle, from the ashes, from the depths of despair and put down the gloves. Love waits. It is NOT held captive. It is NOT far from your reach. It is NOT over there, somewhere else far away.

It's right there! Stand apart from conflict and chaos. Stand radiant. Stand tall. Stand in the peace of God. All there is, is LOVE!   xoxo

I read "Peace to my mind. Let all my thoughts be still," recently. In this world, to have a peaceful mind, being still is necessary. The noise of the day can consume you, exhaust you, cause you to lose your way. Your workday, hours with the children, retired aloneness… can be exhausting.

You must be *intentional* about finding your peace. Be *intentional* about being in a space of rest and stillness in the midst of living in a world where attainment and drive work so hard at grabbing your attention. And all the while be *intentional* in the middle of all that "watching what you're letting into your space, your body, your mind." It matters.

When you look around, do you see bitterness and upset and rage? Do you see negativity and sadness and confusion? Well just because something is OUT there, doesn't mean you have to accept it IN HERE. In here peace can live vibrantly, steadfast and true. In here is where solace waits for you. In here is what counts. You just have to bring it to the forefront.

STOP. Notice the Love. Receive the Love. Share the Love. Live the Love. All there is, is LOVE!   xoxo ❤

  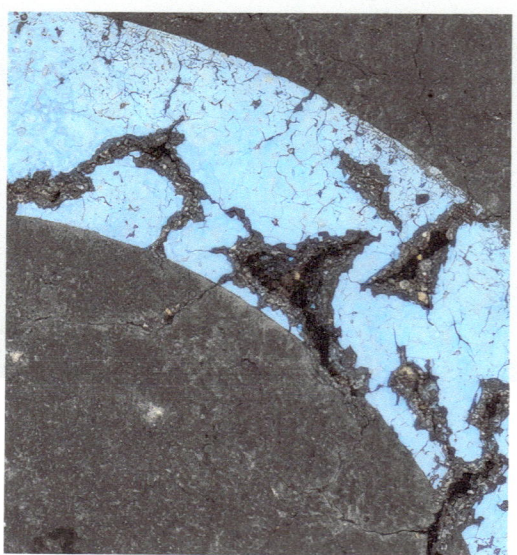

I love LOVE. I love coffee. I love crisp fall weather. I love walking in the park. I love my chocolate protein pudding. I love the smell of a burning candle in another room. I love sitting in my she-zebo at the crack of dawn on a glorious morning with my coffee listening to nature. I love when I see people smiling while sharing their passion for life. I love finding a dime in the most obscure places. I love when my phone rings and it's my mamma. I love putting on a pair of pants on a 'I-feel-fat-day' and they fit! I love when a stranger holds the door for me. I love when I find a heart where I never expected it. Did I say I love coffee and I love LOVE?

What do you love? Take time to sit and think about it. If you have time, grab a pen and jot some down. If you feel eager, share them with a friend, a coworker or a sibling? And if you feel bold, at the end of the day read your list out loud to yourself with a huge gratitude at the end.

All there is, is LOVE! ♥ xoxo

There are times when love cannot be explained. It cannot be justified. It cannot be measured. It just is. It glows from the inside of us. It wells up from the belly of our being at the most awkward of times, the most exciting of times, the most grieving of times. It shines a light on others who have never seen it like this before, those who may need it most.

When we're looking for it... or not... it can just show up in the oddest of places. Places where love never lived. Places that were darker than pitch black. Places where a barrier was built up so thick and so high that no human could tear it down. Places where it's tough to recognize it.

That's where God's LOVE comes in. His love is unconditional. It's all encompassing. It's for everyone at any given time, in any given moment. JUST BECAUSE. You don't have to earn it or do anything to capture it and you don't have to tuck it away for safe keeping. When your judgement, expectations, frustration, anger and upset, are all gone, when the old stories, bad habits and lies of the enemy are released ....guess what?

All there is, is LOVE! xoxo

So come on, my soul Oh, don't you get shy on me

Lift up your song 'cause you've got a lion inside of those lungs.

Get up and praise the Lord!! — "Gratitude" song lyrics by Brandon Lake

…..THIS. This right here. Brings a joy to my heart and a pep to my step. As I was walking the park, listening to this song I couldn't help but play the air drums and smile from ear to ear. People may have seen me and thought… "Is she okay?" I would've yelled back…"Oh don't you worry about me, I'm better than great." On that day, I listened to the song over and over and over, reflecting on my life and embracing the beauty of it.

I don't have much fit for a King, but my Hallelujah. Yet IT IS ENOUGH! AND He loves me even still. SPOILER ALERT… He loves you even still.

…..THAT. That right there. Is where my love comes from. His love gives me strength to endure, compassion to serve, courage to press on, faith to go around the mountain one more time and truth to know that my life has purpose. And what about you? Where do you get your love?

All there is, is LOVE! ♥ xoxo

"We must have more faith in the power of love to eternally renew itself than in the power of fear to tear us asunder." – Marianne Williamson

Can I get your vote? If push came to shove, where would you land?

Would you stand on the rooftops shouting about the power of love, miracles and greatness or would you march in a parade spreading the power of fear, anger and hate?

Think on that. I truly hope you decide on the power of LOVE.

Life could be lovely, blissful, simple and more harmonious for you. It could make sense without thinking too hard about it. Things would fall into place. Doors would open. Books would fall at your feet. Answers would appear. All because of the Power of Love. Give it a try.

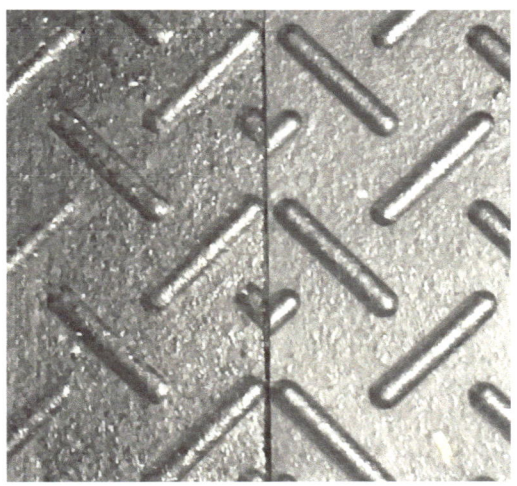  

Do you ever wonder if your aloneness could turn to loneliness which could turn to sadness which could turn to depression which could turn to tragedy. Hm? That's where my mind goes after living through the suicide of a loved one. A beautiful life turned to tragedy in a nanosecond.

Yet in that same breath we could sit in our aloneness thinking of the things that bring some joy, some happy, some giggles. The corners of our mouths perked up a bit with a smile beginning to form. We can rest in the stillness, the quiet, the slow beat of things around us and find solace, tranquility and wonderment in what being alone can bring us.

Alone doesn't have to be lonely. Love doesn't allow that.

I sit reflecting on the desires of my heart letting the tears fall, I declare once again…. Although the cavern is dark, the road is narrow and the journey is long… I am brave, I am loved and it is well with my soul. Let's live in the silence together and sit in each other's quiet aloneness. xoxo

All there is, is LOVE!

How's your heart? How's your love? Is it vibrant, brilliant and glowing? Is it overflowing with fervent wonder and explosive joy to share with the world?

If you look radiant and stunning and handsome on the outside what good is it if your heart is spoiled and dirty and rotten? Make sure your outside shines like your inside. Make sure your essence inside and your demeanor outside match. Be sure not to walk around with a gallantly framed suit of clothes fit for a king or queen, smiling at the world, acting all put-together and on top of the world, and all the while have a disgruntled heart at the core.

And the love that you share should not be dependent on who is seeking it. If you have a hard time with that, maybe it's time to learn a new way of loving, which means unlearning what you think you already know.

All there is, is LOVE!

Nothing is missing. Everything is present. It's all within you. Already.

Can you see it? ... If you can't see it, it could be that you're looking too low? Or maybe you're looking TOO HIGH? It could be that you're sleep walking in your own illusions. You've been operating a certain way for so long that you've grown accustomed to it and you can't see the beauty and the wonder that lies outside the comfort and the perception... which – SPOILER ALERT - you created.

You may have created it out of survival or out of wanting to belong or out of fear of unknown outcomes. Whatever the reason is, if you dive deep into it, you just might learn that you don't need life to be that way any longer. That you can rise above your past circumstances. That you can change the direction of your journey. That you can learn something new. That you can live a life of tenderness, humility, compassion and love.

All there is, is LOVE! ❤

There are days when my heart is so heavy and all I want to do is relax into the tranquility of my yard. My soul is filled with a reverence that nature can quickly bring. I sit with the sounds of the birds and the faraway train. I like to reflect on how blessed I am and run through my mind all the things I'm grateful for. I think about the greatest part of the day and how God's Goodness has poured into my life again and again and again. And as I sit and ponder What Now, I'm reminded to release my pride, my stories, my burdens. I simply stand in the gap between 'what was' and 'what can be.' I stop to be present between the already and the not yet and as I've said before… I'll head around the mountain one more time.

This time with JOY and LOVE!

Won't you join me? All there is, is LOVE!

What 4-letter words did you wake up with this morning?

I hope one of them was LOVE.

All there is, is LOVE!

When you're willing to let go of the limits that you've placed upon love, and you're ready to change the way you look at all you were taught about it, and you're done with mundane living that causes it to vacate.... LOVE will show up in the most unlikely, unplanned, unthought of ways.

Open your heart to it's coming. It's on the way. IT is. Melt into the possibility that it's yours. It's there. It's here. Already. Always.

Put the suffering aside. Give up the reference to any past pain. Reject the thoughts of dismay. Rebuke the stories that aren't true. Rekindle a heart that longs for more. Love is part of who you are. Love has been there since the beginning. Remember? Forgive your wrong doings and just be.

Just BE. Be in the quiet. Be in the now. Be in the resting. Be in the love.

You are Love. All there is, is LOVE! xoxo

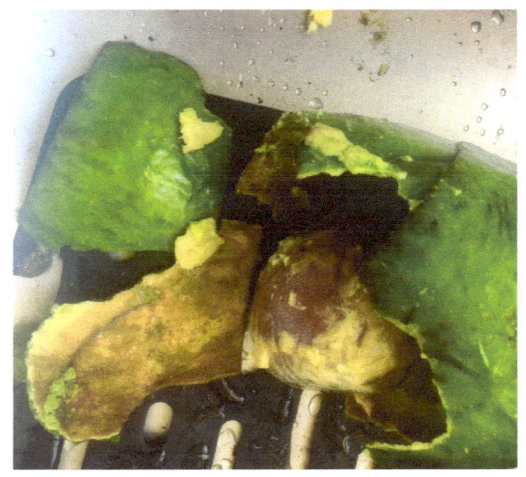  

We who are now the messengers of God, receive His messages. For that is part of our appointed role. *"He needs our voice that He may speak through us. He needs our hands to hold His messages and carry them to those whom He appoints. He needs our feet to bring us where He wills, that those who wait in misery may be at last delivered. He needs our will united with His Own, that we may be the true receivers of the gifts He gives."*
— ACIM Lesson 154 11:3–5

Are you someone who will step into the space created for you to serve others? Is there an opportunity right in front of you to love another at this moment? Can today be the day you forgive someone for an infraction they probably aren't even aware they set forth? Will you go beyond the place that stops you, to do more than last time? How about the way you speak, walk, lead, follow? How can you be the bigger person in this situation you find yourself in? Are you ready to be a vessel? How about the planter, the waterer, the sower? How can you be different today?

Yes, even again.

Go. Be bold. Go.

All there is, is LOVE! ❤ xoxo

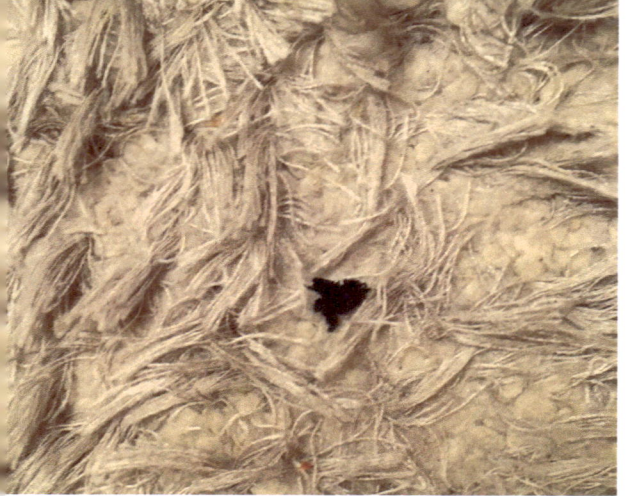

Prepare yourself for love today. Prepare your mind as you step out the door. Be ready to give whatever you've got. Prepare your words, thoughts and actions to come from the deepest, strongest, most assured space of love that lies within you. Feeling nervous about it? Then maybe for today, crack open the window to your heart, sweep away the cobwebs in the fear-filled spaces and use a tad of that hidden love. Lay down the angers, hurts and jealousies. Set aside any assumptions and judgements.

BE intentional to love whoever crosses your path today.

BE the beacon of what can be in the world.

BE the gaslight in the dark part of someone's day.

BE the safe place for another to return a smile as they walk on by.

BE a blessing by your presence, just because you can.

All there is, is LOVE! xoxo

The love of God is nothing like the love of the world. His love is eternal, unconditional, deep-rooted, unmeasurable, luminous. His love is always there, spreading out, freely given. His love is ready for the lost, the found, the wanderer, the chosen.

If you come to Him with any preconceived notions…beware… you won't receive something new or anything you haven't yet experienced. You'll receive exactly what you preconceived about. You'll call it what you were looking for. You'll have it labeled before it even shows up.

Imagine… if you went fishing with a friend and you brought your best catfish rod and you did not give up the way you know how to release the line nor how to reel in the fish. And you didn't hear the instructions from your friend with the fly rod. Well…. You will not learn a new way to fish. You will not be able catch salmon or trout. You will not be open to receive a fresh new idea. Give up what you think you know and fish in a new way, with a new tool and a new outlook.

Back to the love, give up what you think you know about love, give up your ideas and opinions of how it does or doesn't work, remove the barriers and love in a new way. The world's ways are not His ways. AND since we're here, living in it with its ups and downs and the lures of the enemy … we might as well LOVE. All there is, is LOVE!

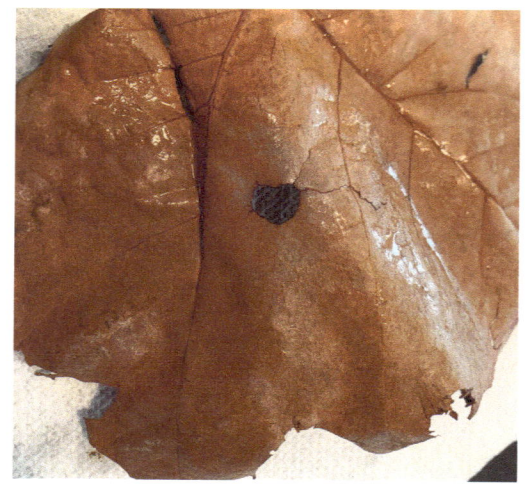  

Have you heard of the Law of Gravity? How about the Law of Attraction? Law of Elasticity? Of Buoyancy? Of Partial Pressures? I could go on. There are so many Universal Laws that are in motion all around us. Without our help.

These Universal Laws describe or predict a range of natural phenomena. Whether you understand them, study them, are aware of them or just live with them unknowingly… they are there. Period. You cannot make them happen and you cannot stop them from happening. They just exist.

So is the Law of LOVE. It exists. It is. Period. Love is steadfast, constant, congruent, changeless. There is no limit to love. And just like all the other natural Laws…. You cannot stop it. You cannot control it. You cannot prevent another from loving you. You cannot avoid its presence.

Can you see it?

Can you hear it?

Can you feel it?

It's there. All there is, is LOVE!

Love. It's always on my mind. What about you?

I often daydream that if there was more love in the world, I truly believe there would be far less sadness, homelessness, dis-ease, loneliness and suicide. Any and all tactics of the enemy come to us as negative fear filled characteristics and if we rebuked them, instead of inviting them into our vocabulary of storytelling….. there'd be far less of them and so much more caring, compassion, understanding, joy, forgiveness, kindness and …love.

Love is ours to share. It resides in us. YES… in US.

And it's up to us to share it.

So the next time WE come against an angry thought, a fear-filled motive, a bad bad BAD choice, WE must search our heart. Where is the love? Go past what you're afraid of. Look beyond what others might think. Be stronger than the one mocking you. ..and JUST LOVE.

All there is, is LOVE! ❤️

This morning on my drive to work a little red car was moving from lane to lane, faster than the rest of us. They clearly had somewhere to be and they were getting where they needed to be quite quickly. The thing about this downtown is…. in 'The Fort' …. the red lights turn to green in sync. In sync when cars travel the speed limit. Not the road runner speed. So at the next traffic light this car would get there first, and then they'd have to wait for it to turn green because they got there too fast. At one point it weaved in front of me and it appeared they were going to hit me… so I tooted my horn… did they not see me, I thought. Phew, that was close! As I rolled up to the next intersection, the driver was yelling at me. I couldn't hear what she was saying. The little girl in the backseat stared at me as this woman proceeded to give me the finger. My heart was sad. Sad that she had so much anger in her heart, sad for whatever is going on in her life that she would react this way and sad that her baby girl sees this kind of reaction to the world. I did all I could to sit in love and not react back. To just love this unknown traveler and pray that she gets where she's going safely. Sending prayers and LOVE her way. BE the love. xoxo

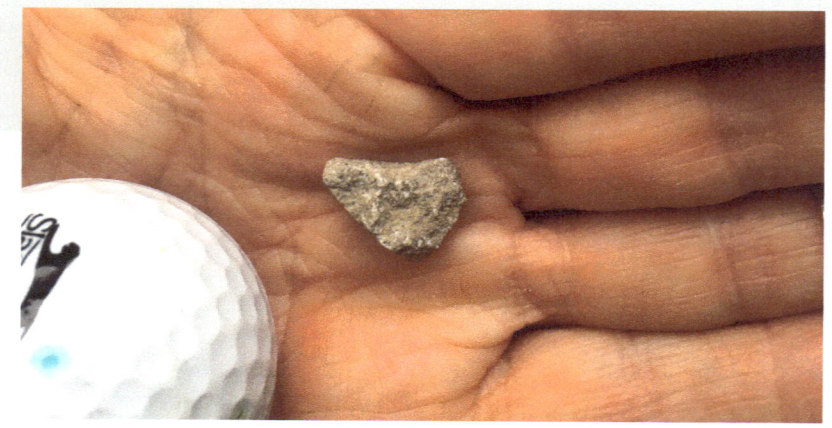 

Love cannot come into a heart that is full of fear. Now... that fear could very well appear real because of what occurred before. Fear from what was done or said or mishandled in your life, before. BUT... the past is gone. It is over. It is only alive in your mind. In your memory. When you talk about something from yesterday and you repeat it over and over and over again, that speaking about it keeps it real. You speak as if it is SO by constant storytelling. And because of that... it will continue to show up. You may even find evidence to back up your past situations and justify them all day long. Telling the world "SEE? I told you!"

Change things up..... start to speak into the love that is buried, since way back when. The love that is hiding in the attic of your heart, the love that seems to be gone, the love that feels so out of place. It is not gone. It is there! It always has been. You were born with Love. It is innate in you. It did not go away, it just might be covered up by years and years of pain and hurts and burdens.

It's like a deer who loses its antlers or a snake who sheds its skin. Release and let go. Let go of the story of what was, the story engulfed in fear and upset... so you can be free to experience the love that is beneath.

All there is, is LOVE. xoxo

I was reading about forgiveness this morning. There were a few insights that I GOT. I mean I really got them. *BOOM* Like a megaphone announcing the next athlete.

A few of them created a little tension in me. Whenever this happens, I know there's something to look at, on the inside. My heart was torn. So, I read it again…. and again… and again… each time a little slower, relaxing my shoulders and unclenching my jaw and breathing deeper.

"Forgiveness must be practiced - it is alien to this world."

OK, GOT IT.

"Do not look upon the sinners with guilt and condemnation."

Huh? What?

This one had me stop and think of a whole lot of my "BUTs." BUT they did this, BUT they said that!!! BUT. Then upon further reading, I GOT IT…

"Would I condemn myself or my loved one for doing THIS or THAT?" NOPE. I would beg for forgiveness. I know I WOULD! There laid my epiphany… I decided to practice forgiveness still, with a softened heart, breathing deeply into all of it. REMEMBERING… all there is, is LOVE. xoxo

Just because I don't agree with your choices, love your decisions, take on your ideas… just because I don't cheer you on, run the marathon with you or march in your parade.. just because you wear 8 different colors at the same time and I wear black… just because you're NOTHING like me… yadda yadda yadda….all of these DO NOT MEAN I DON'T LOVE YOU.

As I age.. I've come to love myself more and more every day and in THAT I've learned to LOVE others. It's been a long, judgmental road. A road of persecution and blame, guilt and shame. But GOD!! I am SO BLESSED to have done and still do THE WORK to be my best self. Ever Onward my friends. Ever Onward on your journey of JUSTs. All There Is, Is LOVE! ♥

With love in you, by you, beside you, filling you up, pouring out of you... you can do many things. You have unspeakable power. You are attuned to a higher calling. You are the bearer of humility. Serving and giving are the side effects to having a foundation in LOVE. When love is present... fear, pride and ego disappear. There is no pretense, no defense and there are no illusions. There is no upset, no chaos, no drama. It is purely, simply, matter-of-factly LOVE. All day.

It is powerful. Step out with Love. Just LOVE. I don't know any other way to say it. Let go of all the ridiculousness that keeps you wound up in terror, misery, smallness. Whatever it is that fear does to you. Let go.

Deep within, there is only LOVE. It's time to share it with others!!! Sure it's scary... what will people say, how will they respond, how can you even go there? Start by praying. Pray for Love to win. Pray for Love to be the backdrop. Pray for Love to fill your heart. Pray.

The words and the steps will come.   All there is, is LOVE

xoxo

Is this you? You hide. In the dark. Alone. Shut down. Shut off. Isolated from others. Falsely protected in your space. Ignoring anything good. Sitting with a content and comfortable mode of survival. Alone. Did you know it is in the hiddenness where life frightens us most?

Is this you? You aren't even sure how you got there, but it feels safe. You shrink further into isolation and separation and swallowed up by more darkness. In that space there is no light. There are zero words of encouragement. There is no hope of joy. There is only an illusion of cozy.

Do you have a skewed understanding of a fight not worth taking on? Where aloneness turns to loneliness and engulfs everything and the fear increases, keeping you concealed from your own desires to break out?

Come out. Come out. Oh brave one. Come out.

There is no darkness that light cannot dispel.

There is no fear that love cannot overcome.

Love is real. Love exists. Come out.

NO LIMITS. I just listened to a podcast and it inspired me to think about having no limits in my life. There are no limits to what we can do. WE are the ones who put limits on ourselves. We stop ourselves in our tracks; delaying action, running our racket, giving excuses, living small.

Where do you stop? Are you scared, do you listen to negativity, believe in your failures, enjoy lunch with the opponent? Are you tired, complacent overwhelmed? Whatever is stopping you is your self-taught limitation.

SPOILER ALERT: There are No Limits that cannot be overcome.

If you change the process, find a new way, invent a different outcome, talk to another person, go the extra mile….. you just might go beyond where you used to stop. Where you saw nothing, now there's something.

Instead of doing a thing for the money, power, accolades or popularity… instead do it because you LOVE it… now that will take you far.

YOU put the limit on yourself. YOU can remove it.

Always LOVE! ❤

God is Love.

We are Love.

When WE recognize that God is our supply and His supply is limitless, bountiful, exceedingly and abundantly more than we could ever think or imagine and WE embrace that God is love, then we will know like we know like we KNOW, that all the love in the world is ours.

Period. Exclamation point!

WE will then live from a place beyond our current thinking. The thought patterns 'of this world' are far different than the thought patterns of His.

When WE choose to take our eyes off of the satisfaction of the ego, the enemy, the pride… of this world, AND LOOK at LOVE…WE will see…..

All there is, is Love.

It's right there, can't you see it! xoxo

What's on my mind? LOVE. Love. Self-love. Sharing love. Agape love. Little bits of love. HUGE chasms of love. Momma love. Baby love. Love in a Hallmark film. Love from a greeting card. Love in a fortune cookie. Love on a wedding day. Love in the locker room. Love love love. It's pretty much on my mind all the time. It's what gets me out of bed. It's what makes my world go round. It's what keeps me going on a really bad awful kinda day. It's what I think of at night when I hit the pillow.

Where's your love showing up? What brings you love? How do you create more love? How many kinds of love fill your cup? How can you express your love with others?

You got nothin?!!! Wait a minute. What? It's in there. Is it blocked by sadness, attitude or unforgiveness? When all your barriers to love's coming are removed, love shows up. And on that day...watch out! You could bring love into all your situations, expand your heart and bring light into a world of darkness.

People wouldn't know what to do with you. They better watch out because there's more where that came from!! LOVE!!

 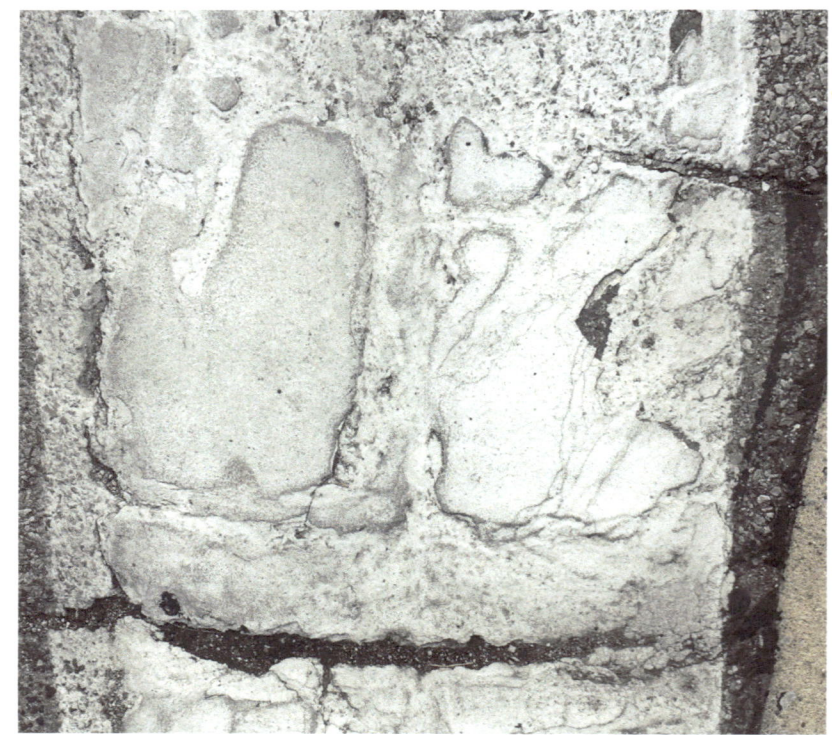

Love is what you get when laughter fills the air between friends.

Love is what you get with the hug from an elder who won't let go.

Love is what you get when hearing a child's giggle at a playground.

Love is what you get when you live your life fearlessly.

Love is what you get when you embrace the beauty of who you are, the precious gift that you are to many and the difference you make in the world.

LOVE is what you get!!! ❤

When you least expect it... When you've got your mind on something else... When you're on a roll getting things done... When you're working a plan for a specific result... When you're busy doing what you're doing...

...then a heart shape sighting can take your breath away... do you see it?

Does it remind you of a time in your life that was overflowing with love? Is there a nudging of sorts to reach out for loves sake? Are you reminded of the LOVE of a friend, a neighbor, a coach, a teacher?

It's under your nose, in your eyes, touching your skin, gasping your lungs, pulsing your heart, giving you goosebumps. It's RIGHT THERE.

Please tell me you know it, that you want it, look for it and you will see it!

May LOVE show up for you today. xoxo

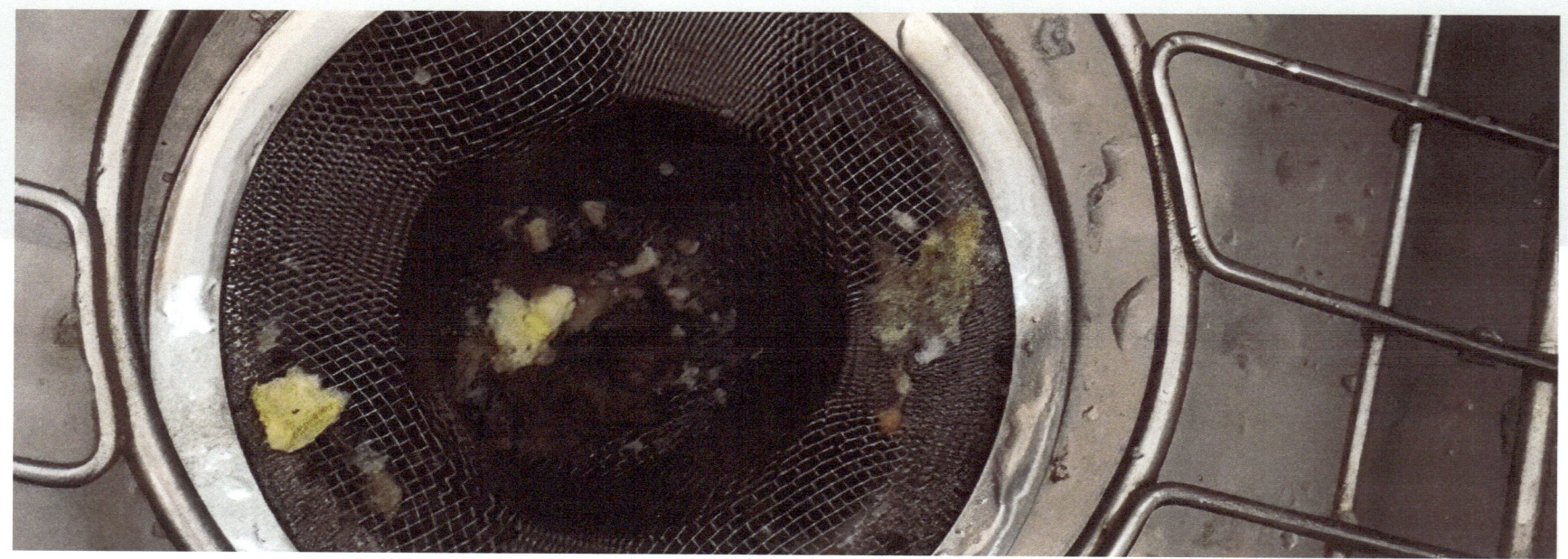

Maybe today. Maybe you. Maybe me. Maybe now.

LOVE has a way of bringing out forgotten memories, inviting hellos, renewing friendships, captivating our attention and creating playful laughter. Love has a way of taking our mind off our problems.

BUT.... it also has a way of bringing out deep sadness, feelings of I-wish-this-was-over, neglected kinships, rejected relationships and uncertainty.

As you go about your day remember to share a smile with a stranger, be intentional with your conversations and offer more love than you normally would to a neighbor. Say hello to a stranger, visit the desk of a coworker, lend a hand to an elder. You could very possibly be the only light in the day of someone's darkness.

While you're at it, treat yourself with kindness, find a few things you're grateful for and go outside to be with the earth.

ALL There Is, Is LOVE   xoxo

There are areas in my life where I am accomplished, renewed, enjoyed, empowered, restored. Where I feel on top of the world. I'm an overcomer, wealthy, prosperous, gifted and blessed.

There are also areas in my life where I am rebuked, rejected, uninvited, ridiculed, disregarded and judged. Where I must remind myself who I am.

I persevere. I press in. I stay the course. I'm tired but I do the next thing, anyway. I put one foot in front of the other, regardless. I look at NOW and notice what it is and respond with "OK."

I'm in a season in my life right now that I'm not too keen on, but it's the season I'm in. So, here I go. I give myself a pat on the back. I pick myself up by my bootstraps. I do what needs doing right here. I give all I've got to those around me. I persevere with joy in my heart.

What gets you going and keeps you going? What do you tell yourself when the going gets rough? What do you give your time to, for a refueling?

May you have what it takes to stand tall in your spot in the world. xoxo ❤

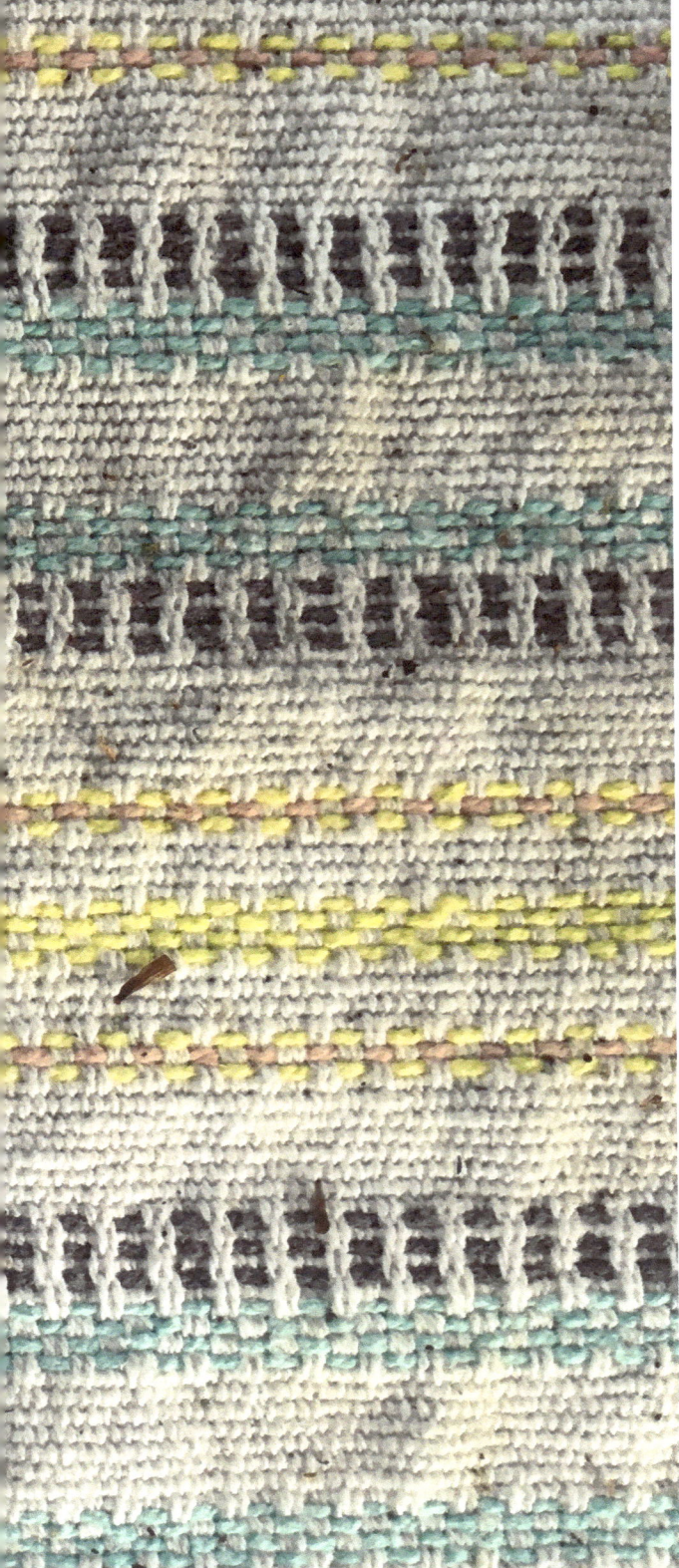

Our minds are so much more powerful than we may ever imagine, know or understand. Why is that? Why do we limit our thinking? Why do we get scared and stop? Why do we mistrust the blessing right in front of us?

Could it be because the enemy doesn't want you to know what your God-given SPIRIT knows? The enemy is sly at blocking your power, desires and dreams and filling in the gaps with lies.

Oh and they aren't always ugly lies either…oh NO… some are all sugar coated, glistening with a shiny glow and drawing you in with the most powerful lures. And sometimes they come to us from sources that we love. Be alert. Be aware. Pay attention to the thought patterns running around in your head, the words that come out of your mouth and how you spend your time. Do not be fooled by the enemy's tactics. Stay sharp.

Want to change what IS? You've got to do the work. Start with LOVE>> ♥

When you are physically in the dark, you cannot see the light.

When you are emotionally in the dark, you cannot feel the love.

What? You don't believe there's another way, other than this dark place? Then you surely will not perceive anything different. You will look and find and hold onto what you want to see as truth so you can declare it to be so.

Light and Love exist even if you deny them, even if you don't experience them, even if you've decided to stay in the comfort of the dark.

Light and Love IS. They didn't go away. They wait patiently for your return.

If you can muster up the courage to take a teeny glimpse outside the darkness... you'll see and then you'll know... the way of love is yours.

Always love. xoxo

Our mindset is not set in stone. Neither is our intent or our promises or our wishes. They're all made up, created by us. Our stories, our history, our knowledge, they're all created by the thoughts in our minds.

We have the ability to recreate them, along with our intent and promises and wishes….we can recreate what's so. We can learn something new and change what's already there into something we desire. We can bring new ideas, thought patterns, habits, speaking and dreams into fruition. Into a concrete reality.

It takes freeing the mind of what we think we already know.

For Real! xoxo

 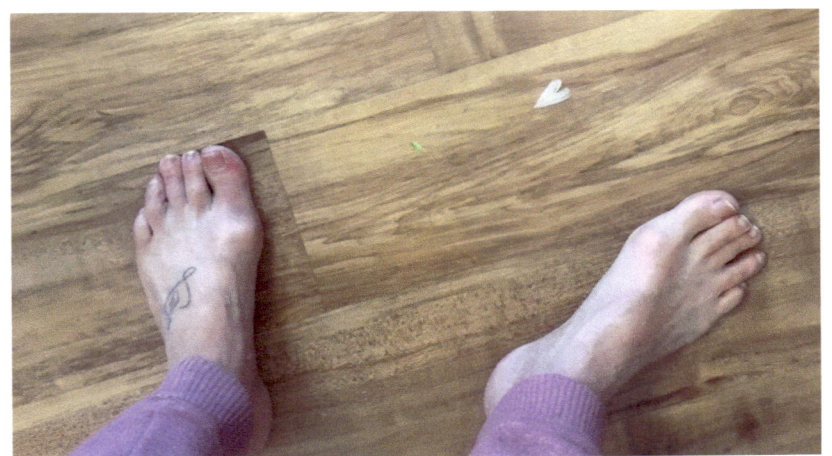

Everything you see is a result of your thoughts and if you don't guard them, they can switch from loving to fearful faster than you can say Supercalifragilisticexpialidocious. Thoughts can change in a matter of seconds! BAM... like that! Do you live with a miracle mindset and believe that you have the capacity to change your thoughts? Try it.

    Deciding what movie to watch? Comedy? ...BAM... Suspense.

    Wondering what to wear to work? Khakis? ...BAM...Jeans.

    Trying to make up your mind about lunch? Tacos? ...BAM...Salad.

Now try it on your automatic thought patterns. Master your thoughts with all you've got! Think of a scenario where you can change your immediate response to something.

Talking negative to yourself? ...BAM!....say something nice.

The kids are getting rambunctious.? ...BAM...speak soft while direct

Feeling uptight from a long day? .... BAM!... just love!!

All there is, is LOVE. ❤

 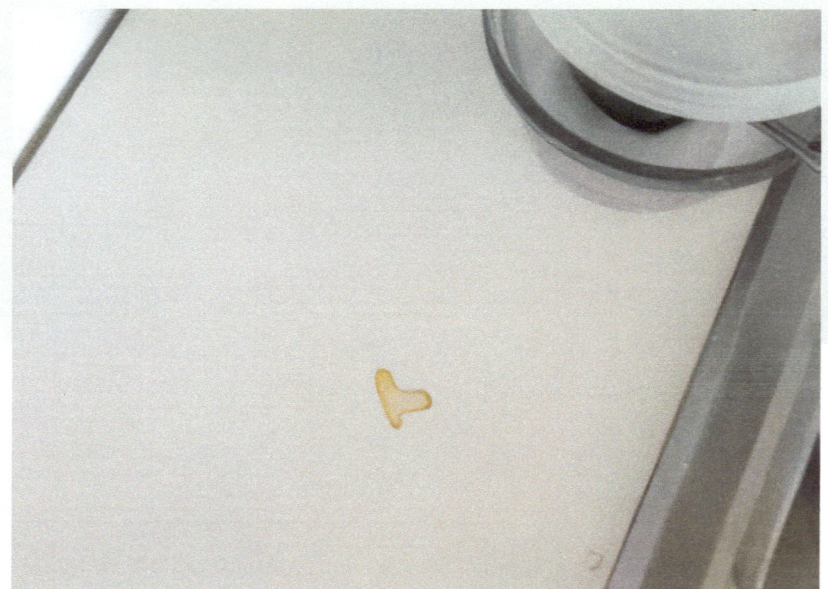

Your perceptions create your relationships to be the way they are.

If you perceive through fear… you will judge, you will ridicule, you will blame. If you perceive through love… you will invite, you will compliment, you will go with the flow.

Work hard at leaving your baggage at the doorway of a new relationship rather than carrying it in there with you and showing it off as if it's still existing. It is a story of something that was. Stop hanging on to it.

Chances are… it's not real anymore, it's not who you are, it doesn't speak to who you want to be either. It's a perceived idea that you created from a past experience—an experience that has no relevance to now.

It doesn't belong in what's new for you. These old ways aren't for you to carry. You're not who you were then. All is new through you having no past thoughts going with you into a new space in time. Isn't that great?

Be free from the fear-filled false perceptions of yesterday and…just love. xoxo

"Joy in the Sadness" is my mantra these days.

When the consistent beating of sadness and the repetitive habitual motion of joy compete for my attention, it is then that I recognize truth. I choose to stay with them both… not negating or entertaining one over the other.

You see, if I give too much attention to the sadness, I'd never get out of bed. And if I give too much attention to the joy I'd overshadow some teaching moments with avoidance. It is important I recognize and accept any emotion that shows up while I'm walking it out.

I choose to live with them both, teetering between them, living in the vulnerability of the moment, ebbing and flowing, walking the narrow path.

Will you choose to look for the "Joy in the Sadness?" I'll meet you there.

All there is, is LOVE.

On my drive home I was feeling quite a bit of irritation. Irritated by those who didn't drive right away when the light turned green AND by those who ran the red light AND by those who didn't use their directionals. AND. Then **BOOM** I was reminded of my own shortcomings. "Hello Tracy - Mirror Mirror!" I had to consciously choose to release my upset, to loosen the tightening in my shoulders, to let go the clenching of my teeth and breathe. I had to decide in that moment how to respond.

I live just like those who irritated me. Often times I can be in such a state of mind that I neglect, forget and don't' follow the rules. I'm not being present and find that my rushing thoughts take me away from doing what's best. Best for me AND for humanity. I'm reminded to be kind.

BOOM It all changed. I let the car who was inching their way to go, to pass ahead of me, I waited while the person crossed the street and I relaxed away the overload of the day as I patiently, lovingly, meandered home.

Dang it was humbling to see that my irritation is from my own doing, my own judgement, my own choice. And it felt GREAT to make the moment different. xoxo

Breathe. Release. Love.

Life can be hard. Even on a good day. Remember that! Stay in LOVE.

Division, separation and isolation may be knocking on your door. Stay in LOVE.

Anger, hatred and upset might be yelling at you from every direction. Stay in LOVE.

You can invite them all in for tea and attempt to persuade them into living with peace and joy. You can explain a favorable compromise and ask them to back off. You can beg them to understand the beauty found in silence. They may listen, but they won't hear you. They're not about to be swayed by your love. You see, these enemies of the mind come to you from the devil's playground. Lurking in the shadows. Waiting to pounce.

You can continue to stand in the peace and joy you possess and you can LOVE your enemy from afar. Remember they do not know what they do and you don't have to follow their schemes. Stay in LOVE.

xoxo

Release the opinions of how you think something 'should be' or 'could be' or 'why they did it like that' or 'why didn't they do it like this'.

Your opinion doesn't really matter outside of yourself. It's yours. No-one else's. Others aren't usually interested in anything outside of themselves, therefore they probably don't quite care about your opinion anyway.

If you can release your mindset of one-way thinking, you can open up the space for so much more to show up, to occur, to live with for you. You give room to new ideas and see things from another perspective. You release your ego and open your heart. You give up your steadfast strongly charged egoic thoughts and give others an opportunity to share theirs. It's beautiful to BE this way. To live with an openness in a closed up world. To be one with others.

You are in a space of acceptance, a space of peace, a space of LOVE ❤

What are you filling your body with? Are you filling it up with junk food that keeps you longing for more junk food? Food that does not satisfy the body's nutritional needs? Food that's empty of the goodness of the earth? Food that sends a false strategy on wholeness?

Think again about what you fill your body up with.

What are you filling your mind with? Are you filling it up with negativity that keeps you low ? Stories of chaos and fear ridden ideas of scarcity? Scary movies and violent crime novels that deprive you of peace? Worries and anxieties placed upon you from the world?

Think again about what you fill your mind with.

What are you filling your spirit with? Are you filling it up with false burdens and tempting indulgences which you know don't fulfill? Lies from the enemy that keep you in the dark? Black magic, psychic worship and tarot readings from demonologists.

Think again about what you fill your spirit with.

Today's a good day to start thinking. And fill them all up with LOVE.

xoxo

"We are looking for someone who is looking for us." - Curt Thompson.

Relationships (romantic or not) are the utter craving of the soul. We should intentionally find people who we can connect to, be social with, enjoy commonalities and experience differences. Relationships where we can speak truth, find humor in ourselves, meet each other where we are and add value to each other's lives.

It is up to us to create healthy, thriving friendships that last. We cannot leave it to others to fulfill the craving in our soul. That's our job. If our life is not as we want it to be, it is up to us to do something about it. We must be strong and courageous and go gather others together.

Next time you meet someone who causes you to smile... say hello.

xoxo

Every day I work at loving others. Loving those who sin and ridicule and judge and fail by their own hand. Those who rebuke and gossip and speak highly of themselves, their accomplishments and their possessions. Those who aren't like me. Those who are like me. Those WHO ARE ME.

Every day I work at loving myself. Loving me with my shortcomings, my judgement, my ignorance. Loving me with my sins, upsets and failures.

Every Day I'm reminded that Love holds no grievances, that ONLY love is real and that ALL there is, is LOVE.

May each day's lesson bring us closer and closer to LOVE. Drawing deeper still to the heart of the matter. Looking beyond what others bring to the table and staying true to our calling. xoxo

In "The Chosen", Season 2/Episode 2, Phillip introduces Nathaniel to Jesus. They're having a conversation and Jesus proceeds to say things to Nathaniel that nobody would know — except God. Nathaniel looks toward Phillip with shock. Jesus says, "Don't look at him, look at Me" and finishes the conversation with, "Follow Me". Nathaniel never expected that!! Did he think to himself. "Who? Me? Are you talking to me?!!"

THAT would have been my reaction. Who is this man who knows these things? It can only be God Himself AND He asks ME to go with HIM!?

May we (yes....I'm talking to me here) keep our gaze on HIM... not at our child, our brother, our neighbor, our parent, or even ourselves. May we keep our eyes on Jesus as we walk this earth, this fallen world.

And in the meantime... May we just LOVE. Even when it's hard. Even during attack. Even when things don't look the way we wanted. Even when someone says something we never expected.

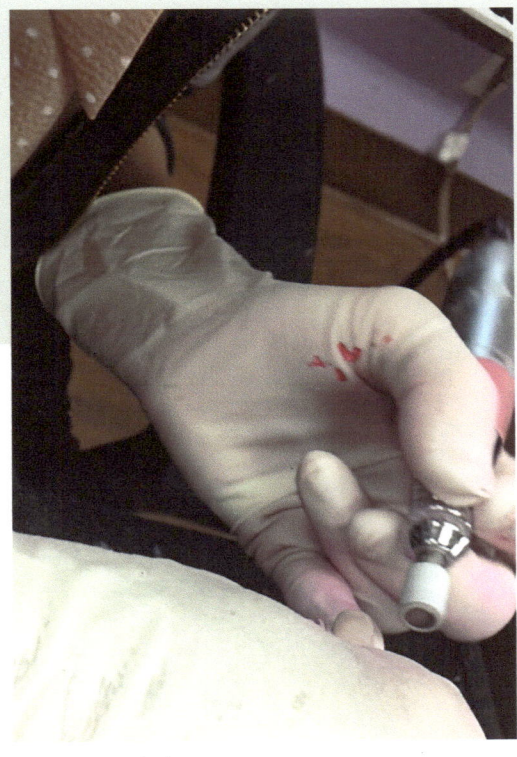  

If God is Love…and God is in us…then Love must be in us. In you. In me. Everywhere. Now THAT'S the best news ever!!! Let it out people… Let it out!

Don't be afraid. Don't be terrified. Wrap yourself in a blanket of courage. Arm yourself with an inner conviction of certainty. Step out into your day with a new vision, a new mission, a new purpose.

Be the very difference that you look for. Be the beacon of compassion you long for. Be the example of goodness you desire. Dance in the rain of goodness as it sprinkles upon your day. Let out the silly happies that have been filling up for a good belly laugh.

Share it with all the people in your path. Just because you can! ❤️

The road is narrow and the journey is long.

Remember that!

Do not deter, do not lose hope. Grab your lunch and go!

While on your journey, you'll pass Iamnotenough Avenue. Turn right onto WhatifIblowit Street and follow that for some time. At the fork in the road, ignore the alluring landscape of Allkindsofmistakes Valley on your left and then turn right down the dusty path of Loveisallaroundyou Road. If you're feeling tired and want to stop for a break, you can relax at the Miraclesabound Reservation and dip your toes into Lake Blessing.

I cannot imagine a day without hope to get me through. I do not know what my life would be like if I didn't keep on the narrow road. I am filled with gratitude and love. Pressing on. Doing the next thing. Sharing love. xoxo

Did you really think that you were uniquely and wonderfully made as a child just so later in life you could deny your true self just because it might be off-putting to someone else? Seriously? Why would you do that!? Why would you let someone else dictate your worth? They don't know you. They don't know your design They don't know your gifts. They cannot measure your talent. Take back the yardstick you gave them!

If someone is put off by your greatness, 1st of all — that's on them AND 2nd of all — I feel sorry for them. They have no idea how uniquely and wonderfully they're made. You see, if they knew, they'd be cheering you on instead of tearing you down. They'd see they are you and you are them.

You are made for a reason and a purpose. Do with it the best you can.

And always loving those around you. They're doing the best they can.

xoxo

"THE FELLOWSHIP OF THE UNASHAMED" – Unknown Rwandan Man

A young man wrote this the eve before he refused to deny Christ to his tribe. They weren't keen on his heart's desire and death was their answer.

"TFOTU" brings goosebumps to my skin and shivers to my spine. It fills my soul with a fervent exuberance that I can't explain. Have you read it?

My favorite part is:

"I am not called to follow others—I am appointed to lead. Life will become a great adventure if I step out to the front line and fight for those who are too weak to fight for themselves. I am not to look back at what I have lost but instead look forward to the great victories that are in front of me. My pain will be turned into passion to change the world around me. I am to remember that the fight is not just for me, it is for those I love."

May we be the difference in someone's life because of the fire in our hearts, the fire in our bellies, the fire in our souls.... to love.

xoxo

  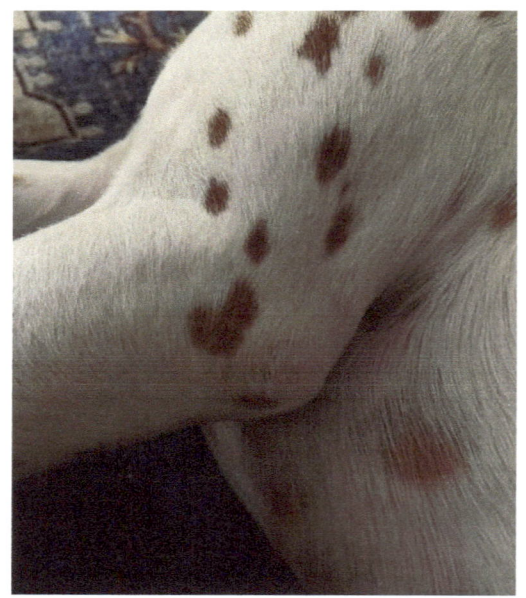

Along with a list of things I've read about what people hunger for; within relationships, partnerships, work….
I've read that a man craves that his thoughts be respected and a woman desires that her feelings be cherished.

man-crave-thoughts-respected —— woman-desire-feelings-cherished

In many ways we are very different, men and women. Yet in other ways, we are the same. Both want to be heard, accepted, longed for and LOVED.

Can we put down our list of needs and serve the other? Can we put away our defenses, our righteousness, our intellect and in be in a loving space with others? Can we release the ego and pride and come from a place of giving? Can we see beyond what's staring back at us in the moment?

At the core of it ALL…. All there is, IS LOVE. Ever Onward my friends. ❤

xoxo

God's LOVE is relentless. It's overflowing, fervently given, always poured out, consistently available and forever ours. BUT... we must be intentional about who we are and how we live.... to be a beacon of love to others.

Have you heard someone say we must love ourselves first?

That statement is too often taken lightly, ignored or minimized. To love ourselves is the most important choice in our life. So.... no kidding, love yourself. From the top to the bottom. From deep inside your belly to the hairs on your skin. All of you.

What do I mean? Be good to yourself from the moment you wake up all the way to the moment you lay your head down, waiting on tomorrow.

How? You could begin with no longer selling out on what fills your soul, no more agreeing with the enemy, stop letting others rule over you, get rid of living in a chaos and drama whirlpool and give up buying into the BS that others say to you. Treat yourself with kindness and say nice things.

Stand Firm. He is here and He loves you!!!!

All there is, is LOVE!

Are you feeling overwhelmed, burdened, dealing with some tough news?

Sound the Alarm.

Do you need help with the kids, your yard, an undone task at work?

Sound The Alarm.

Have you received some great news, want to share a blessing, celebrate something stupendous?

Sound The Alarm.

Our Pastor spoke of Nehemiah this weekend and how when his people Sounded The Alarm, everyone gathered. They came to share the news, hear the news, help each other and stand in the gap with their friends.

If you're not the one Sounding The Alarm… I hope you are answering the Sound of someone else's Alarm. ♥
Be the one who answers the call.

May LOVE prevail in all situations and circumstances for you today!

I often talk about the power of the mind and how we can just as easily take ourselves down a rabbit hole, as easily as we can lift ourselves up and up and up AND change the outcome of what's in front of us.

I often talk to clients about "What you think, is yours and what others think, is theirs." I say that, "You cannot control their thoughts and they cannot control yours. You don't have to like what they think, nor do they have to like what you think." It is what it is. Have you seen that saying?

When you can come to a place of 'YOU be YOU' and 'ME be ME' and love each other in the midst of THAT connected space, your LIFE WILL BE TRANSFORMED. THEN you can 'WE be WE' in the midst of it all.

You'll no longer be at the effect of someone else's cause. You'll no longer be run by your emotions and you'll be released from reactions of others.

All there is, is LOVE ❤

For those of you who are unsure of what to do with the love you have, for those of you who are struggling with finding love, for those of you who are shut down to the possibility of love; I read this in a book somewhere and I use it as a coaching tool with my clients as well as in my own life. I hope you'll add it to your daily mantra regime or mind treatment:

"My task is not to seek for love, for love is everywhere.

My task is to seek all the barriers I have against its coming".

It always goes back to us. We're the one walking our journey out, we're stepping out of the loneliness, we're turning away from isolation, fear and confusion. We're the one believing in ourselves, we're taking on a new day with a new outlook and new hope. We're opening our heart AGAIN. Us. Not them. It's ours to do if we want love in our lives.

MAY LOVE FIND YOU and MAY YOU BE READY.

"Love Holds No Grievances" by Tara Singh is a deep read. One that challenges us to make the correction in ourselves, to always love, and that happiness is independent of all things external. ❤

As you ponder your thoughts about your heart's state of being and answer the question, 'what is in my way of me loving freely?'… can you honestly say that the thing in the way is far more important than having the love?

And if you find yourself pointing the finger at someone else who may or may not have done something to you or against you….SPOILER ALERT… the correction must occur in you first. Still.

Your grievances, your upsets, your hurts are yours to correct in you.

Then you can JUST LOVE. Then you can have an honest open heart to love on others. Then you can begin to see your ability to love and that your happiness in life has nothing to do with anything or anyone out there. Then you can have joy that overwhelms the darkness. Then. Only then.

It's an inside job.

xoxo

I talk about finding love everywhere by the many heart shape reminders that pop up out of nowhere. I talk about the longing for a love grander than any we may have ever known before. I talk about sharing the intimate parts of ourselves to trust that we are worthy to be known deeply. I talk about the vulnerability that comes along with sharing our hearts.

I don't talk too much about the struggles though. I don't talk too much about the angst that comes along with hoping. I don't talk much about the days where loneliness has the ability to overshadow everything else. I don't talk about the gut-wrenching hollowness that resides deep within.

Maybe it's because those sad parts don't stick around very long and when they're thrown in among days of joy, they seem to be too small to even pay attention to or bother with. I choose not to give them my attention.

I'm not sure if I notice love because I long for it so much… but what I do know is, as I give love away versus hide it, I'm given more than I could ever dream or imagine and the sad parts evaporate like mist in the air.

I am blessed by love. xoxo

Stop to notice some love right under your feet. Then stop and notice some love right under your nose. Then, right there in your relationships. Then, right there in your home. Then right there in your thoughts. Stop.

If you're the chooser of what you say and you're the one who picks the words that come out of your mouth, why wouldn't you pick loving, kind and generous ones? There are thousands of words to pick from. Why be careless with what you speak about? Be intentional with your words.

If you're not sure how to get there, how to change your thought patterns, your frame of reference, or even how to show up differently... open the Thesaurus. You can learn new ways to say the same thing. Train your mind, change your words AND broaden your horizon of goodness and love.

Hearts, hearts, and more hearts. Can you see them? They stop me in my tracks every time …. I reflect on love. How can I create it? How can I share it? Who do I need to be to hold it? Who can I give some to?

You can bring love into your conversations, into your work situations, into your daily affirmations and prayers. Actually, you can talk of love in any circumstance, at any time. You choose your words. You choose your response. You choose your contribution. Why not make it all from a place of LOVE?

All there is, is love.

Some days I NEED the reminder more than others. Some days I'm so busy, or feeling down, or being self-consumed, that a heart seriously stops me and causes me to be reflective on what's going on in my life. Am I grateful? Am I content? Am I peaceful? Or am I a grumpy pants growling at anyone for nothing at all? Stop and think—how can you love…?

Well, if I am a grumpy pants, seeing hearts when and where I least expect them, certainly changes that disposition pretty quickly! I'm reminded of how blessed I am. And I am grateful! What about you? JUST LOVE xoxo

Today is a good day to smile in your mirror.

Today is a good day to say hello to someone you don't know.

Today is a good day just because YOU said it's going to be a good day.

You can turn a disgruntled moment into a peaceful one. Like THAT!

You can turn your frown into a smile. Like THAT!

You can turn your forlorn attitude into one of content. Like THAT!

Just like you can physically move from here to there, you can move sad to happy, you can move fear to love, you can move mundane to vibrance.

How will you start your day?

AND how will you end it?

Choose love.

Do you find yourself swimming in Lake Condemnation with the enemy? Complaining about what life dealt you and what you're going through? Are you judging the people around you? Are you causing conflict, upset and discord? "Keep it up," says the enemy as he cheers you on for more!! ......He LOVES when you act that way.

It is in THAT space that we MUST turn our thoughts away from the unruly misguided chitter chatter he continuously jumbles in our heads. SPOILER ALERT.... You deserve to live free from the suffering that you inflict upon yourself. (read that again) Do you find yourself listening to the lies, acting as if they're true, giving them a voice and inviting the enemy to have a seat on the couch? DON'T DO IT! He may look sincere, pleasant and innocent. BUT he's more than happy to join you in your pity party and commiserate with you, reminding you again and again how awful you are. Intersecting vulgarity and ridicule and sinful thoughts at every turn.

But GOD!!!! Remember.... You are the SON of the KING, the DAUGHTER of the KING. Speak the words of truth. Believe in all that God says you are. Live from THAT place. That place of adoration and LOVE!!!!

I BELIEVE....

That God's supply of love is limitless.

That the attitude of gratitude brings prosperity.

That giving causes getting.

That opening the space for good to come in, creates a vacuum.

That good shows up ALWAYS in all ways.

That our dreams and goals—or something better—is on its way.

That forgiveness is priceless.

That there is no order of difficulty in miracles.

That I am you and you are me.

When we focus on being grateful, seeing goodness, sharing kindness and spreading love to our peeps, it creates a happier more appreciative world.

And of all the things I believe......I believe.......All there is, IS LOVE!

Just when you think you're making an easy dinner… ❤

The temptations of the world are very attractive. They give illusions of beauty, success and power. They sneak in and tease us, always showing their best side. They reveal what you could have if you only chose them. They brag of a life that could satisfy all your wants, needs and desires. They promise popularity and recognition and wealth. Don't' be fooled!

You must remember there are consequences to temptations, their satisfaction is temporary and it's most often not all that it's cracked up to be. They attract you into a cycle that you can easily get so caught up in that it grabs your full attention. You feel controlled by it and you just might get to the point where you can't differentiate between the deceit of it and the normalcy of life. Don't be fooled.

If you have a feeling in your gut that you shouldn't, or it's not right or you're not so sure about something….do not let your next thought be, "ohhhh it's just once," "it's only a little bit," or "nobody will know." Stand strong against any temptations that sneak in and beg for your time. Lastly, remember the enemy comes to kill, steal and destroy. Don't be fooled.

Be careful of the temptations of the world and the sweetness it sends.   xoxo

Share the LOVE! Everywhere you go, with everyone you meet, no matter what it looks like, no matter how you feel, no matter what's going on.

Because really, beyond the veil, the mask, the BS narrative, there is truth. Behind the façade, the make believe, the 'I don't trust anyone' attitude that you carry around everyday, there is truth. The innate truth of our inherent God given nature. Our raw, real, authentic, truth. Our loving, kind, generous, happy truth. It is the ways of the world that instill fear, causing us to shut down and resist putting down our façade.

Isn't that tiring? Walking around acting 'AS IF'… all the time. As if you're important. As if you're successful. As if you have it all together.

Have the guts to step out from the myth and be yourself. So many people will love your vulnerability, your assurance, your humility, your love.

Come on. I'll meet you there, in the place where, all there is, IS LOVE!

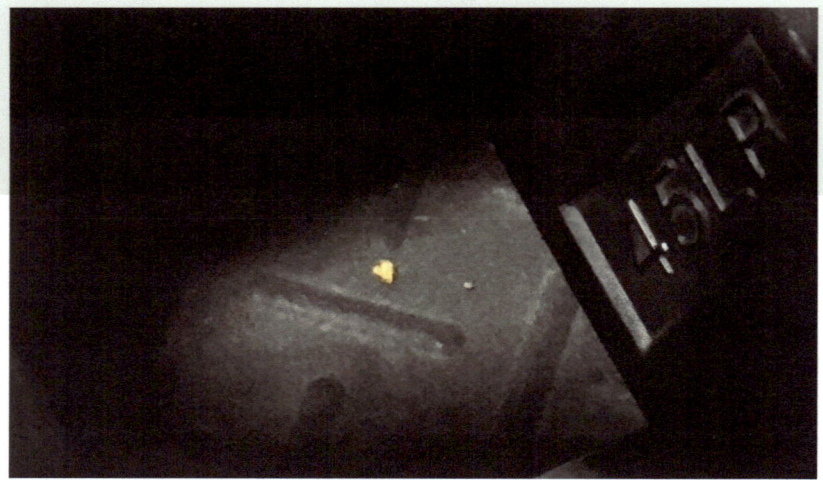 

Love can't communicate through a preoccupied mind. Find that moment where serenity and bliss fill you up. Find that state of being where calm and solace settle in. Find that place which is easily peaceful and untroubled.

Settle into a comfy chair or spread out on a picnic blanket, swing on a tree swing or prop yourself up in bed. Find a place that awakes in you a sense of security and comfort. A restful place where your mind is still.

Then in the silence ask the question.... How can I love myself today?

What do you need to do in this moment, later on or even tomorrow? What is it that you can do for YOU?! How can you love YOU? What will you first give to YOU?

You see, when it really comes down to it... you are your own advocate. You are your own cheerleader. When nobody else is around, all you have is YOU!!! So... start there.

Take a serious account of how, what, when and where you can put YOU before everything and everyone else. Start small if you may...but START.

Then... go love another. ❤

You could see things this way . . .

"oh look, a leaf, a teeny tiny green leaf, that must've blown in on a windy day, sitting still on the sidewalk."

Or you could change your perspective and look from another direction.

You could see things this way . . .

"oh see here now, this cute little leaf is stopping me in my brisk walk, reminding me of love, bringing my attention back to the moment, giving me a halt in time to be grateful."

It's how we see things and where our perspective is, that matters most.

May you see the love that's right in front of you.

It is perfect.

It's always perfect.

It doesn't seem perfect.

It is perfect.

Maybe I'm looking at it all wrong. I have to look inward. Where is my heart? Where is my love? I tell myself to look closer. Look in the rubble. Look in the disarray. Look where I think it's too ugly, messy or forbidden to see. Look in the spaces where unforgiveness lives. LOOK for the love.

Just like this chunk of asphalt that appears to be an unwanted piece of the broken sidewalk, a piece that no longer fits where it once did. Look closer. Look at the bumps and crevasses, the black and grey. Look beyond what your eyes see in the brokenness. Look for the love.

There are teeny tiny rock hearts within them. Can you see them? In the places no one thought to look before. The love that is hidden within. The love that you try to protect. The love that you thought melted away. The love within your heart.

Remember, underneath it all, mixed in it all, on top of it all… IS LOVE!

When we let go of fear so that love can come in, the result is monstrously fabulous. Overwhelmingly beautiful. Undeniably breathtaking.

Within any fear that we carry… there very well may have been anger, hurt, shame or guilt. Maybe some loss or rejection or judgement. Whatever got us into the state of fear, we can forgive and make it right.

Are you so comfortable in the complacency that you've forgotten what 'to love' looks like. Guess what???… In fears absence you'll surely find an abundance of joy, beauty, triumph and steadfast overcoming power!! There are miracles, possibilities and endless sources of goodness. There is grace, victory, blessings and opportunities. There is transformation, restoration and mercy and ohhhh boyyyyy there is love.

Is it time to put down the gloves you use to fight for the fearful thoughts and live in love instead? Maybe? Yes!! Maybe… is a good beginning. ❤

  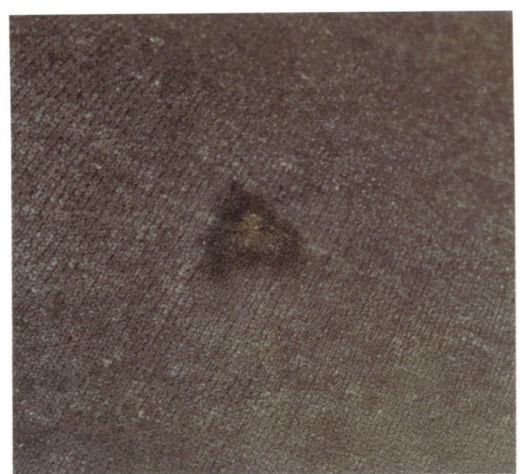

Every upset that I have about a situation, relationship or circumstance, is MINE to deal with. Those are MY upsets about how THAT over there is working out…or not working out FOR ME… with my point of reference, desires and expectations.

MY flesh, MY story, MY reactions that stir inside of ME.

They are MINE to learn from, let go of and realign with love.

I have a choice to make every time I get triggered….. to be bitter or better. There are times when I just want to throw in the towel and become a recluse. (leave me alone people) But then, I'm immediately reminded before the thought has a chance to solidify, that when I DO spend time hibernating and alone…. the enemy finds me and begins to stir the pot of remorse and regret. Which then makes it harder to get up and out.

In that moment, I repeat over and over…Oh Hell No! You see, I REFUSE to let that happen. Soooo I, once again, put on my big girl panties and get on with my life. I continue to release that which toggles me, I rebuke the enemy's efforts to pull me down and I remember that there is so much goodness inside of me to give.

To ME, to YOU, to the world. All there is, is LOVE.

"To bring a relationship to harmony demands the undoing of one's concepts and ideas. It is the undoing that awakens new potentials that will not allow you to limit yourself to your own opinion."
– Tara Singh

Ah, now that is good!

I look forward to a new thought, a new idea, a new conversation. Something that will open my mind to see something differently than I always have. A way of thinking that is unlike the past. A reflection of something that lays beyond where my sight may stop me. An insight or daydream that could possibly show me what I've never imagined as so.

May my heart stay open, my mind expand with excitement, my love be the backdrop while I wait and my ego not be threatened, when it comes.

Then and only then will I be someone I have not yet been.

Then and only then will I overcome false pretenses that I set before me.

Then and only then will I release blaming circumstances for my choice.

Then and only then will I love myself more than I ever thought possible.

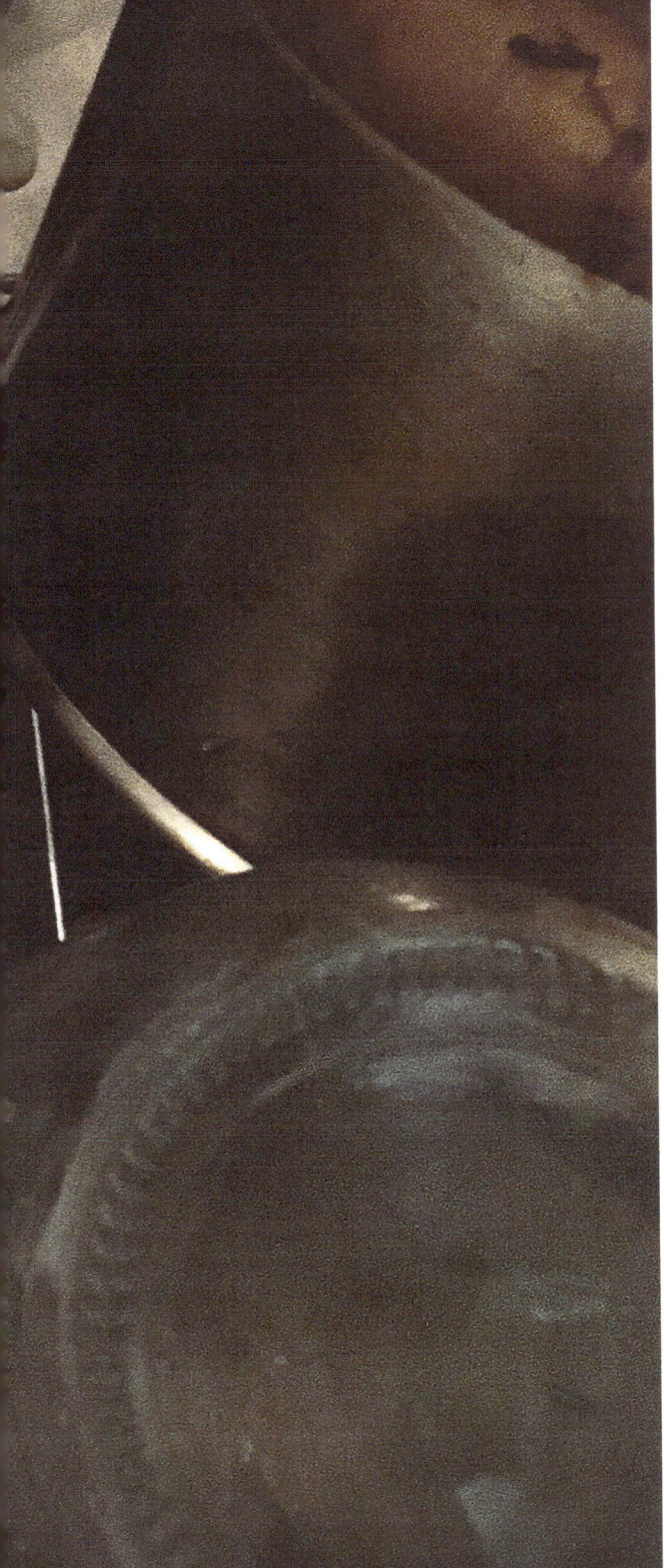

"Mankind's problems cannot be solved externally." – Tara Singh

My problems, your problems, the world's problems are manifested in a material world where egos are appearing as real and acting like the truth. Things have gotten out of balance. In order to solve the problems of the world, we must first start with ourselves. Our bitterness, our opinion, our justification, our judgement. They must all be resolved internally…. so that forgiveness and love can take their place.

I read that bringing one's life into order, living without limiting beliefs, freeing oneself from past conditions, awakening to gratefulness and forgiving ourselves first, is a perfect start to a life of harmony and love.

People ask me how I get along with my son's father… LOVE.

…how I got through the death of my sweetheart… LOVE.

…how I make it through the rough times… LOVE.

I have love because of my parents, yes… and my son, absolutely…. but mostly My Love is from my GOD. It's taken a lot of intentional choices and consistent work to now live with my heart open and my ego tamed… yes, I said tamed because it still exists. Every day.

To see, to capture and to breath in the LOVE that comes from God. I am filled up and overflowing. It is the difference in my life today. My wish in the new year is for all mankind to stop and release all the chaos, the old stories, the burdens and the wounds that they carry. To open up to love and then go share it with the rest of the world. xoxo ❤

What's on my mind? Love. Especially when it catches me off guard. Like this one. STOP RIGHT THERE….. love caught my eye.

Love can catch your eye in the midst of strangers as you watch those around you share affection, care, attention and compassion.

Love can catch your eye in the quiet of the night as you sit reflecting on the day, remembering all the times you listened, shared and helped others.

Love can catch your eye in the woods, on the beach, at the mountaintop when you take in the beauty around you and let it permeate your heart.

May your eyes be open to it. May you never shrink back from your heart, your love, your truth. May you trust the love that flows around you and let it catch your eye! May you know that you deserve the love that's coming your way. May you live from a place of exuberance for life and excitement for what's possible. xoxo

Love is really all that matters. It's a fallen world here on Earth. Have you noticed that? The fallen-ness, broken-ness, chaotic-ness of this place we call home? It shows up in the news, in conversations, tabloids and in social media. It shows up in choices and judgments, in negativity, in gossip and bragging. It shows up whether you look for it or not. It covers the ground we walk on and the air we breathe.

We must know it and be prepared for when it shows up. Because it WILL show up! We must pay attention to the sinful nature, learn to shut our mouths about it and love that which appears to be broken.

Notice I said 'appears' to be broken. It could very well be something else. Is it survival? Is it protection? Is it fear? Is it an old story rearing its ugly head again? Give the benefit of the doubt and rise above the illusion.

One smile at a time. One hug at a time. One heart at a time. xoxo

Love shows up. Expected or unexpected. Hoped for or dreamed about. It especially shows up if your heart is open to it, if your mind is full of it, if your eyes have the vision for it. Do you know love? Have you seen it before? Have you experienced it deep in your bones? Have you been engulfed in it like an oversized blanket on a chilly day?

If you cut into this watermelon, would you have seen the love that lives inside or would you have overlooked it as it stared back at you? You wouldn't have seen it unless someone pointed it out to you? Where else in your life is love showing up and you aren't seeing it?

If you would have seen it straight away, what would this heart have brought to mind? A feeling, a giggle, a thought, a person?

I hope it brings in happy thoughts, little smirks and maybe even a nudge to reach out and say hi to someone.   All there is…is Love. ♥

May love surround you every day. Whether it's from family, friends, yourself or the amazing omnipresent everlasting King of Kings.

May you know the pitter patter of the heart that comes from loving another. May you know the excitement in the veins when you see the face of someone you love. May you feel shivers up and down your spine when you walk side by side with your soulmate.

I pray that however you can experience love throughout your day that you go out and find it. I pray that you step outside the comfort of your everyday reality and bring your love out to the world. I pray that you be bold with your heart and share it with someone, somehow, somewhere.

Can you think of a place, right now, anywhere that brings you comfort and joy? Can you go there (even if it's only in your mind) to be filled up with some feel good, down right awesome happy happy thoughts of love?

May today be the day where you have a glimpse of the fact that...

Love is everywhere and . . . . All there is, is LOVE. ♥ xoxo

When we do what we do in everyday life, like another ground hog day...

when we're rolling through our moments most often on auto-pilot...

when we're moving through our patterns, habits, and behaviors...

it can be surprising and pleasant when LOVE shows up. It can be even more magnificent and fulfilling when we stop and take a moment to reflect on it. Sit in the stillness of love. Reflect on the essence of love.

Stopping in that moment can give us an opportunity to remember all the people we love and who love us. And that we are love! Inside, we ARE love.

While walking out the day, out of nowhere, for no planned reason, with no bugles to bring it in.... love shows up. Alas, my friend!

May we all see, feel and give away the LOVE!

Look what was waiting for me after a rough work day. Now mind you… there are no trees in this parking lot. NONE. NADA! AND the closest tree, …well let's just say the wind went above and beyond in this delivery.

It was so joyfully welcomed at the end of a rough and tough day.

Have you ever had a day when the opponent was working overtime to try and pull you down, but you wouldn't have it?

You know what you're capable of, you know what you're good at and you know what your bosses appreciate about you. And you know NOT to listen to Satan's lies?

This was one of those days where I dug my heels in, rolled up my sleeves and did the hard work. All the do-do-do and go-go-go were worth the love in the parking lot.

All there is…is LOVE!!!! Can you see it!!!!?

It's ALL about the LOVE! Here is yet another sighting. Cooking up the zucchini with some fresh herbs and stirring it all around and WAIT! WHAT!? Yup! You got it right. Love.

When was the last time love showed up for you? Whenever it did... I sure hope you let it settle into your heart, that it put a smile on your face and that it provoked some gratitude and self-loving thoughts.

This love reared its beautiful head in the midst of a very busy day. A meal prep day. Followed by gym bag and work clothes prep for another tomorrow. Because heaven knows if I don't have everything ready for that 5:30 alarm, I won't get out of bed. I'll find too many excuses to stay cozy under the covers dreaming whatever dream has my attention.

Thank God I'm reminded why I do this, how much I matter and that this act of self-love is worth getting out of bed for. All there is, is LOVE. ❤

You can't make this sh*t up!!! I'm indulging in the most wonderful meal and unbeknownst to me I spill salad dressing on my shirt..... well I did know I spilled some... but... I had no idea that it would drip into a heart! ❤️❤️❤️

Do you get it, that when a heart shows up where there isn't usually one... it is a crystal-clear reminder that LOVE exists. EVERYWHERE. ALWAYS. And it is up to us to see it. It is up to us to create it. It is up to you to share it.

In the bright and shiny places and in the mirky and messy places. In the chaos and sadness and in the calm and happiness. Love exists. It exists in all places, in all ways, always. Stop and look. Do you see it?

May your day be overflowing with goodness, gratitude and lots of LOVE!

ALL THERE IS, is LOVE!

The miracle of love is that it lives in all of us. Every single one of us. And it's a choice to make. Our choice. We can choose to love or not. We can choose to hide it under a bushel or share it with the world. It is our choice. The moment we put our feet on the floor in the morning and that last motion of laying our head on the pillow at bedtime. We choose.

If someone was to ask you what/who/how do you love, would you have an answer? Would you have words to quickly roll off your tongue in an eager and joyful response? OR would you grumble at the thought of it, reflecting on misery and upset? Thinking "Augh who needs love, bah humbug!" You have a choice. What will you choose?

If you have squabbles and complaints about how things are going, choose a new outcome through love. If you are hurting and sadness seems to be your best friend, choose a new disposition with love. If you sit alone and seem to think your world is an island, choose a new move in love.

When you least expect it, in the unknown places, even the dark corners of your world... love shows up! Choose LOVE.

When you were out and about, minding your own business, walking and thinking and enjoying the solitude.... Where you jolted *BOOM* out of your thoughts, stopped in your tracks and reminded of love? I believe that if we are to notice it in our worldly view, it is because it lives in our hearts. I believe that unless you are loving and know love, you won't see it no matter how hard you try.

I was enjoying my evening walk, the world around me, my goodness and the fact that I am able to do all that I do. How blessed I am with great friends, an amazing son and a simply fabulous life. I was enjoying all of God's creation, reflecting on life and drinking in the peace and quiet of nightfall. *BOOM* Right under my nose. Of all the leaves that could have been sitting in my chosen path, were these heart-shaped gems.

What a reminder that the earth is connected to the body. That what we require is ALWAYS present. That God is good ALL the time. And, that all there is, is love. ♥ xoxo

"You'd better bring your good gloves," I always say. Be ready! Be ready for the rough and tumble that will be thrown your way. Be ready. If you want to live a life full out, a life with integrity, honesty and truth. Be ready. We're going to go through some tough times. Some rough times. People are going to disappoint you. Situations are going to throw you off course. Stuff is going to happen. It just is. SPOILER ALERT: We live in a fallen world with an enemy who will do whatever it takes to devour us. To take us down. To land us flat on our backs. I'm talking flat! Without warning. Be ready!

Where's your heart!? You cannot drink from the cup of the world over and over again and then expect God to be your right-hand man. It's not going to happen. You've got to drink from His cup, live with virtue and character and boldness and you must stand against the lies of the enemy. You've got to walk away from that which ruins you. It's gonna take some gumption. It's gonna take some grit. It's gonna take a strong back bone. Be ready!

What do you say? You got your good gloves oiled and ready?

All there is, is LOVE. ❤

Why does one have to cause another to lose so that they can win?

What makes one think others should be blamed so that they can appear blameless?

How does one acquire a need to be right so badly that they find someone to make wrong?

I think those are all fear-driven, ego-boasting, flesh-driven decisions that people make. Instead of focusing on how one can serve another, they think of serving themselves first and then if there's anything leftover, they might consider sharing.

Why is it so hard to walk around with mud on your face, or let someone else shine brighter than you, or sit down and listen to the story of another without chiming in?

When we put love first it prevails over all the fear-filled thoughts in our mind, it takes dominion in our heart over any barriers that keep love at bay and it outshines any darkness that's trying to brag some more.

Love IS the stronger force. Love IS the humbler position. Love IS the answer. All there is, is love! xoxo ❤️

Where your mind is, so is your heart. And where you are in your consciousness, it has everything to do with what you see in your experience, in your life, in your world. ……..Heavy stuff right there!

This is written in guru books, metaphysical blogs and The Bible.

If you have a sense of affluence, a sense of omnipresence, a sense of Jesus in your life, you are going to place that on everything you see. Your God-centered seeing has a formative power and it will change the way you view things.

The same is true for negative thinking, ignorant living and bad choices. You're walking down the wrong road if you're looking for a good life.

I know that where I am intellectually is where I will be physically. I know that the frequency in which I thrive from, is the place my life will settle into. I redefine myself daily, releasing burdens and barriers that my ego owns. I am intentional about my time, energy and habits.

Today, I choose love. I choose my words. I walk with goodness.

Won't you do the same?

Love is often hidden by unforgiveness. Especially to the Self. When shame, blame and guilt get in the way, it can be difficult to see the Love that's underneath all the rubble. The lies we hear, the burdens we carry, the traumas we've endured, oh and the negative self-talk we repeat.

If that's how it is for you, I pray that you have the stamina, courage and determination to face all the whatever-it-was that got you there. I pray that you boldly forgive yourself for any wrongdoings, any distorted perceptions and any down right rotten spoken words.

Okay so let's say something really did occur and you wish you could take it all back or have a do-over, BUT you're not sure how. Then, instead, you do nothing and you find yourself walking around with remorse filling your soul. THAT, my friend, is the enemy keeping you stuck, taking away your worth, shutting up your voice, alluring you to self-condemnation.

It's time to make amends and correct the mistake. There's no space for regrets. There's no room for punishment. There's only forgiveness! Look inside, past the false projections of the enemy. Go deep, if that be the case... and while listening to the voice of God, find a speck of love and feed it to yourself. Over and Over and Over. Hold yourself prisoner no more. You are free. xoxo ❤

When you wake up with a grunt or a groan before your feet even hit the floor…

When you get to the office and feel disgruntled before you even look at your email…

When you snap at your child before you get a sip of your morning coffee…

When you lay your head to sleep and you're crying before the song plays 5 notes…

These reactions just might be indicators that you require a little bit of forgiveness today. A few more hugs from a loved one. A little more love today. Love for you, love for them, love for the world.

And YOU'RE the one to give it. Yup. YOU. Dig deep people. It's in there. It might be covered up by illusions and deceptions and burdens… but it's in there. Get rid of everything in the way and go share the love. xoxo

Are you in the middle of a mess? In your bones, in your heart, in your gut? Something that has you in a tizzy, running around in circles? Are you finding yourself avoiding it and filling your moments with something other than dealing with it straight on? Are you praying and hoping that it will go away? SPOILER ALERT: It won't change unless you change.

Just like a messy room. You can turn the light off so you don't have to look at the mess, but that doesn't mean it's not there anymore. It's just in the dark. You can look the other way too, all day and hope it leaves… but it won't unless you do something to make it happen. And just like the physical mess… your mental mess can hide in the dark being ignored in hopes that it changes. If your attitudes, habits and rituals have got you down in the dumps… trust me….. it is exactly as you let it be.

I must say… First — it's going to be ok. Second — you'll get through this. Instead of sitting in the dark, turn on the light, tap into the love and get to work. You'll be sooooo happy you did. ….. All there is, is love. ♥

You cannot see the miracle behind the grievance because it obscures your vision. It diminishes your hope. It hinders your trust. You might think a miracle is waiting for you, but you're not really sure. You want to believe there is one, but this grievance has you so wound up you can't think straight. You remember a time when you had a miracle but you're just not so sure there's another one on its way to you.

Imagine the clouds in the sky on a dreary day. When you are here, with your feet on the ground, looking up.... that's all you see. Big dark gloomy doomy cumulonimbus clouds, possibly bringing in a storm. It is dark and there is no sunshine in sight. But there's another view available.

When you're on a plane and you rise up and up and up... the middle of the same dreary afternoon, above the clouds...the sun fills the sky. Much brighter than you may have ever imagined. The sun was always there, but from your view on the ground, you couldn't see it. SPOILER ALERT: Once the clouds pass, you'll see the bright beautiful glow of the sun. Right there. Same as the miracle. It's there, you just can't see it from where you're standing. Behind the grievance. The difference between the cloud and your grievance — you can't control the cloud.

You get to make a decision. To stay all caught up in the upset OR come at it with love. You choose.   xoxo

When you think about love, what stirs in your heart? There's so many emotions linked to love, I couldn't possibly list them all. Love could be an expression of energy and excitement like a glitter bomb exploding. OR it could be that of renewal and beauty like a butterfly emerging from a cocoon. OR it could be filled with recoil and pain like the piercing of a dagger thrusted into a bullseye. It is as different for each of us, as the many different stars in the sky. What's your LOVE like?

Your unique understanding of love and the story you tell about LOVE is a result of your unique past. Yours. Nobody else's. So don't let anyone tell you that you're wrong for thinking what you think or feeling what you feel. It's yours!! Now if you're not feeling very cozy with the word LOVE, never mind the expression of it YET you want to trust it and express it, believe me.... you can create something new in that arena. You can!

The LOVE you hold in your heart is from yesteryear's memories, journeys and experiences. It's made up of all the failures and successes, hurts and joys. All that others taught you. All that you watched and clung onto. All that you read, heard and lived. All of THAT! AND today is a new day. You have the power to start a new way of LOVE. My hope is that you experience LOVE with feelings of comfort, compassion and pleasure. And if you don't... I pray that you have the ability to change any upset around it, release any lies surrounding it, and courageously embrace it when it shows up.

LOVE is all around. Let's open our eyes to it. Let's open our arms to it. Let's open our hearts to it. All there is, is love.

Awareness. Consciousness. Knowledge. How is my life this way? How am I who I am? What occurred in my life that this is what is so?

Assumption. Illusion. Perception. ….What did I pick up along the way and keep close to the heart? Which teaching impacted my journey? Who spoke into me and what did they say that I grabbed a hold of?

Expectation. Prediction. Anticipation. ….Where do I draw the line between you and me? Where were things set up in such a way that I'm not present? Who threw their gunk on me over and over and over?

Narrative. Story. Reality. ….What was going on that I chose these habits and boundaries? How did I learn my habits and behaviors? Where did I give my mindset so much power?

When I look through a lens of fear, I find that remorse and regret rear their ugly heads and try real hard to remind me of things that are not true about me. BUT BUT BUT when I look through the lens of LOVE, all I can see is peace and joy. There's room to breath and move and create something different. There's space to create happiness and gratitude. There ares reminders everyday, everywhere… that all there is, is Love! ♥

Do not indulge the ego by listening to its attacks on truth. Look beyond the perceptions, illusions and appearances marketed throughout the world. In a world where fear is a cornerstone, things appear to be solid and working for everyone. But with so much homelessness, depression, hunger, disease and suicide, something is NOT working.

A lot of things aren't working! We are separated more now than ever.

Look beyond the veil. Have the courage to go against the rhythm ruled by the darkness. Go beyond the worldly ways and recognize what you can do to make a difference. Dig deep into your love and happiness and give some of it away. Heck... give it all away. You will be filled back up again by The One who fuels you.

God is good. All there is, is love!!!!

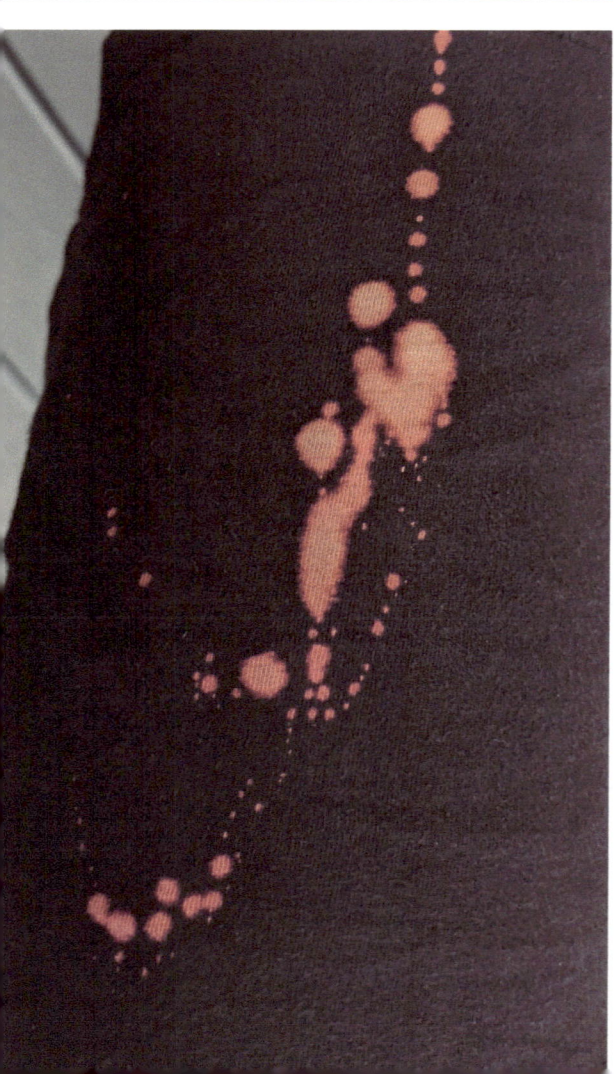

Just when I thought I healed all the internal judgement, thought I unlocked all the shackles of my illusions, thought I released all the barriers from their grip on me... I am met with MORE. Another judgement that I put upon myself. A judgement that protects me — or so I thought. With a justification that explains it — or so I thought. With a story of reason and reckoning — or so I thought.

In that moment of MORE, I'm shown what I've hidden. Hidden between "Go for it girl," and "Wait, it's not safe." When I stay in judgement, I see my ugliness, I'm reminded of the pain, I hold onto hopelessness and I begrudge all loss. These judgements aren't the truth of me. MORE. I don't need MORE.

As my chest rises and falls with every breath I take, as I wipe away my tears with empowerment... there is an emptiness, a letting go, a sweep of bliss that I haven't felt for a long time. This epiphany moment is a place where transformation occurs.

The bricks I've laid that 'falsely' protected me are being washed away like a sandcastle in the rising tide. With each action of forgiveness. I am free.

All there is, is LOVE. xoxo

Boundaries.

Boundaries set in love.

Boundaries set in love are worth setting.

Boundaries set in love are worth setting for each of us.

Others may not like them. Others may call you rude, mean or uncaring. They may rant and rave about how ridiculous you are and throw accusations and question you with their assaults.... What on earth are you doing? Who do you think you are?! How dare you!? ...and a plethora of other things that come up for them as a result of you setting boundaries for you!

Do not be dismayed. Do not be altered. And DO NOT erase or move your boundary. If they don't like it... that's on them. If you set it in love, from the deepest part of your heart with an intention of being loving, you go ahead. You stand firm. You put on your good gloves. You tell yourself how proud you are of YOU. You step out in love.

Boundaries can be tough to implement. But when you love yourself enough to know what you deserve and you know what you will and will not accept, you WILL attract others who declare healthy boundaries set in love too. ❤

 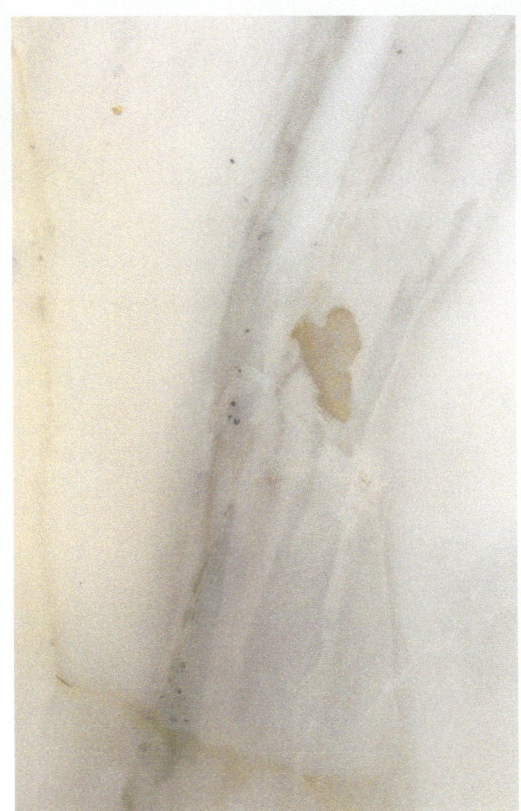 

I believe an open, honest heart is the way to inner peace and love. We share our heart with others because it is what fills us, fuels us, oozes out from us. It feeds them, lifts them up, changes their view. Our heart is one of our most precious possessions and even though it can withstand a battle of sorts, it can reject attacks and it can survive ridicule... that doesn't mean we have to live with that as our state of being. Sure... the love the heart holds can be misunderstood, feared and ignored. You could be rejected, wounded and left with sorrow... that doesn't mean you have to accept the dismissal of others as a true story of who you are. That is their fear. That is their arrogance. That is their perception. Stand in your love and peace, your courage and triumph, your creativity and joy and go share your heart. All there is, is LOVE. ♥ xoxo

We see in other's what we choose to see.

This can be a good thing when we are looking with a loving, and forgiving heart. We can see beyond the judgements, perceptions and illusions that others (or even WE) may have put in the way. When we come from love we have a tendency to see the Truth about a person, even if they cannot see it themselves. When we come from a pure nature with no separation, we can join with others and stand in a place of possibilities. We can see their sinfulness and we offer forgiveness because of the love we carry.

Enlightenment surrounds them and freedom from bondage begins.

Yet, when we look with stories of the past, righteousness and ridicule, we see another's sinful nature and act as if it the truth of who they are and sometimes we go to great lengths to remind them of that. We give no room for change and growth. Forgiveness does not live in our heart…. there is no room for love because fear and anger are taking up all the room.

Be reminded that through the love and forgiveness of self, we are able to love and forgive our brother. When all we see is wrong and blame and malice…. it is time to clean up the mess that resides in our own hearts. That is the Truth of us, and that is where love begins.

We see in other's what we choose to see.

xoxo ❤

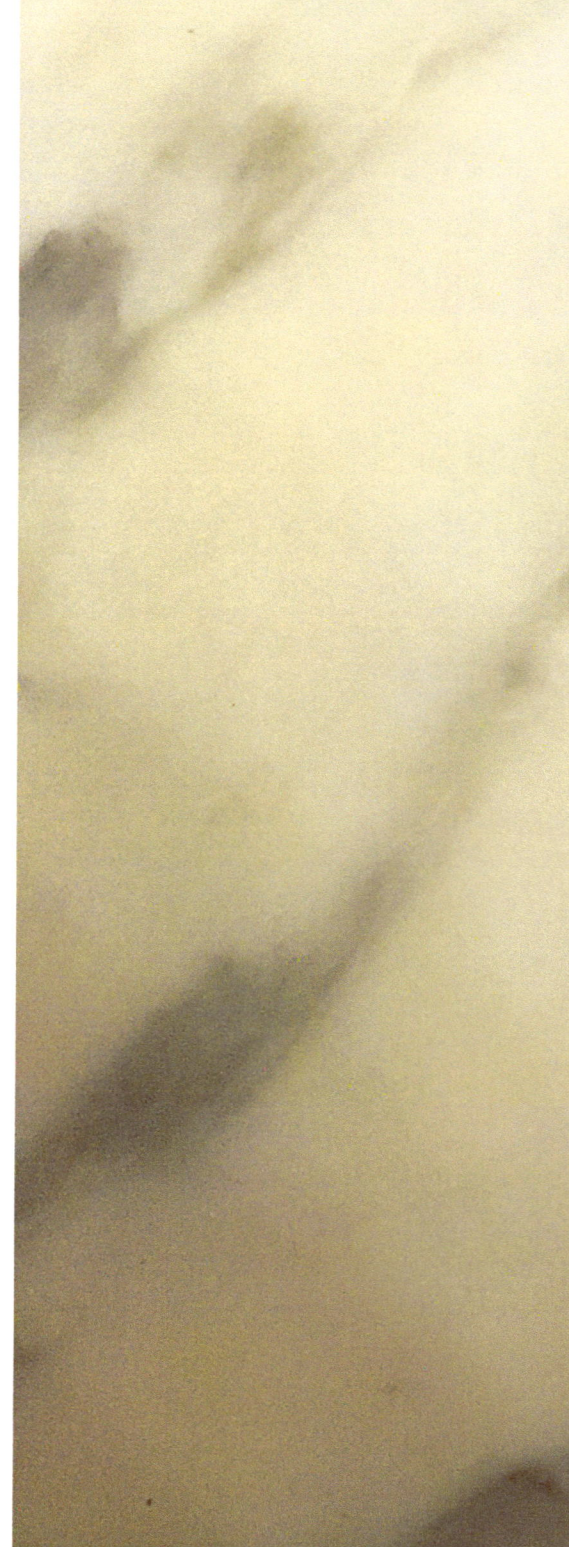

Give LOVE to another.

What?

You're afraid?

Do not be afraid my friend.

Only in giving will you receive. To keep your heart all closed up and hidden away, protected from a time you thought it was broken, will only keep it bleeding. Just like a cut on your body, your heart has the ability to heal.

You must bring it out in the open, pulsing and expressing and healing. Let it scar over as a remembrance of your warrior spirit, your trust in restoration, your ability to let the past go and live in the moment. Let it remind you of all the blessings, miracles and triumphs you have in your life. Let it remind you of when you were scared but you did it anyway.

Give your heart again, you will be amazed at the joy you create in the life of another. xoxo

Errors in your relationships are caused by separation, selfishness, perceptions of loss and many more reasons of your own doing.

Only when "those" are worked out and corrected IN YOU, will your relationships be healed and whole and full of loving attributes. Look within and see…. What is awry and off kilter? Where do you have self-judgement and ill repute? Where are you not being honest with the truth in your soul? Where do you deny yourself for the accolades of others? Where are you saying yes when you mean no? Where are you getting upset with the person or circumstance that you put yourself in, like it's their fault?

Do not punish others because you will not look at and correct your own errors and wrong doings. Take away the shackles and chains that you put on them. Remove the judgement and condemnation you assigned to them.

Be courageous. Look inside. Replace all your fears with love. Miracles abound! Possibilities exist. You are forgiven. You are free. Now go love!! ❤

The world is full of opposites, also known as antonyms. Dark/Light, Black/White, Ying/Yang, Left/Right, Above/Below. I could go on and on and list at least 100 sets based on a search I did. The one I hold close to the cuff is Love/Fear. I work at staying on the side of LOVE. I find myself sitting in it, being it, sharing it, speaking it, however it can be expressed. That's what I live for AND what I want around me, 24-7. LOVE. Not only because love is so wonderful, full of joy, thoughtfulness, positivity and enchantment but also because I DO NOT want to live a life where fear is at the helm. I lived there before... NO thank you!!! It was debilitating, threatening, limiting and life was full of confusion, isolation, deception and darkness. ...Today... I choose LOVE. In my walk with God, I'm reminded that I AM LOVE, fully made from His LOVE, equipped to share it with the world. And so are you. Do not listen to the lies of the enemy, do not sit alone is your sadness, do not buy into the negativity of someone else. Rise up. Reach deep. Shine your light of LOVE with yourself and then go share it with someone else.

Take Heart, YOU ARE LOVE. xoxo

Do you have a nugget of love that you're afraid to share with the world, so afraid that you wrapped it up real tight and stored it away in the depths of your heart? In a spot where no one ever visits, a place that's deep in your darkest darkness? You built a wall around it and put a lock on the gate that surrounds the wall and you keep a watch over it day and night to ensure it's still hidden?

How's that working for you? You see, what happens when you do that, when you protect your heart's love and don't trust to share it is, that no love can come in either.

In your protection of its vulnerability, in your desire to keep it hidden, in your need for its safety… you shut out the love of others. The gentleness, kindness and goodness of others. You block anything that can add to the rejoicing of your life. You cannot see what is waiting on the other side of your isolation, survival or ignorance. You cannot see the love that awaits you, the love that is yours just because, the love that's available to you.

YOU…the one who deserves so much more than what you think possible. Cut off the lock, open the gate, break down the wall and bring your love to the light. It is needed in the world. You are needed in the world.

All there is, is love. ♥ xoxo

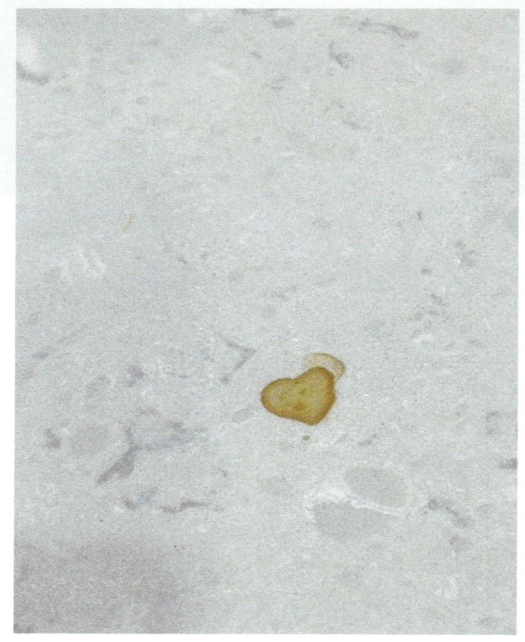  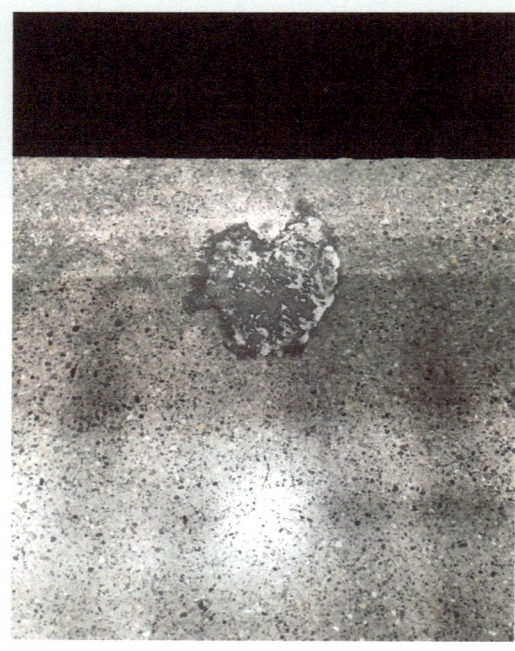

Has your heart been saddened by the loss of a loved one and others around you don't understand the depth of your sadness. Do they question the love you lost? Do they disregard what you're feeling or say things about how you're acting? Why won't they meet you where you are? Sometimes it's because of their own fears around loss or they don't trust anyone but themselves, so they control all situations. Watch out for doing that yourself because when we get caught in controlling situations… we're not enjoying the love that shows up. While you're going through your grief and sadness… remember to embody life and work through the emptiness that's left behind now that this person is no longer on earth. You're really able to hold onto the love you shared AND let it go of the sorrow and grow into a new space for yourself. While you create a new space, find love from others. Until you decide to be the generator of love in your life. There's no pointing the finger or waiting for it to come from someplace else. It's really up to us. To step out of our loneliness and sadness and grief and let go of the steering wheel of control and trust like we did when we were children. Be IN each experience that shows up. Every Day. IN every moment. All there is, is LOVE. ❤

A lot of people have big loads they're carrying on their shoulders. All I can do is stay in a place of compassion and love when I come across someone who appears to be heavy burdened. The other day a gentleman was crossing the street and he seemed to be staring right at me with a face of disgruntlement. I wondered what was going on his life that he was so bewildered and carried what looked like aggravation. Was it because all he had on was a t-shirt and the wind was blowing profusely or was it that his socks were soaking wet because he got caught in the rain or was it that he just received some bad news for himself or a loved one? It saddened me to see him like that and I thought, maybe it was frustration over his circumstance. I gave him a nod and smiled at him as he proceeded to cross in front of me. I've had disgruntlement in my life, I've been frustrated with outcomes and have been dealt a pretty bad hand and have had to work it out. I intentionally chose joy in the middle of the madness and it was not easy, to say the least. But it was necessary for my soul. Absolutely necessary. I sure hope on those days when you'd rather just throw in the towel and live in the frustration, that you have the strength to love. Love yourself. Love another.

Just love. xoxo

As the book comes to an end, may your heart be happy and overflowing with joy and may your plan for your tomorrows include all the greatness and excitement you can possibly bring in. Endings offer opportunities to look back so we can plan ahead with insight and knowing. We can look back on the good, the bad, and the ugly, and ask ourselves some pertinent questions for self growth, soul growth, life growth. As we sit in the questions, we allow the answers to be revealed. We may be reminded of things we neglected, forgotten or walked on past. Not sure of what to ask?

Here are some ideas: What worked and what didn't work, what goals did you meet and which ones did you not, what relationships were encouraged and which were released, what habits did you add and which did you let go?

Also, think about: what new things you tried, opportunities you took on, invitations you accepted, places you visited, things you gave away, areas you served.

And we can't forget to reflect on: how you treated others, where you put your health first, and how good you were to yourself. With all of the reflections stirring around in the crockpot of your mind… come up with some ideas, goals and habits you can bring into the new day so you will be a better version of you. And Just Love!

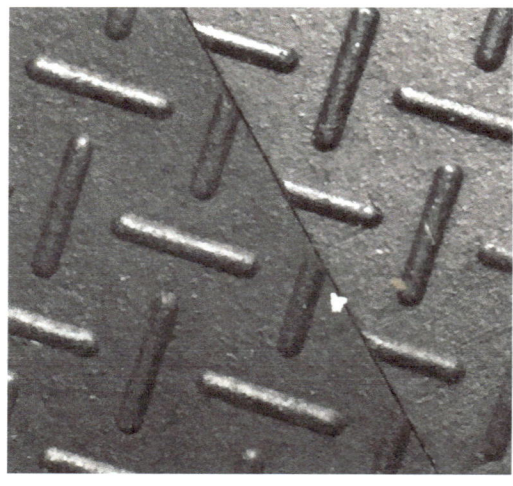  

Quote References:

15 – Marianne Williamson, *Illuminata* (New York: Random House, 1994), 157.

25 – *A Course in Miracles: Combined volume* (Foundation of Inner Peace, 2007), 289, lesson 157.

59 – Curt Thompson (@curt_thompsonmd), "We are looking for someone who is looking for us," X, January 18, 2022. https://x.com/curt_thompsonmd/status/1483409010351120389?lang=en

67 – "Fellowship of the Unashamed," unknown Rwandan man. gospeltruth.net/unashamed.htm

91 – Tara Singh, *Love Holds No Grievances – The Ending of Attack* (Life Action Press, 1988), 9.

93 – Tara Singh, *Nothing Real Can Be Threatened* (Life Action Press, 1989), 247.

Photo Title/Credit:

1 – Looking at the Love Dish/me

2 – Beach Blessing/Molly Jackson • Love Remains/me

3 – Water Drop Romance/me • Beets & Sprouts/me • Spiderweb Catch/me

4 – Lovey Dovey Palm/JulieAnn McDougall

5 – Stomp Your Feet, please/me • Barrell of LOVE/me

7 – Sitting with the Love/me

8 – Citrus Find/me • Wipe up the Love/me • Sandstone Stand Strong/me

9 – In the Center of it All/Tracy's anonymous friend

10 – Beach Walkin'/Molly Jackson

11 – Teeny Tiny Find/me • Leafin Love/me

12 – Hot Cocoa Bubbles/me • Raisin the Love/me • High Road/Cara Pinnick

13 – Rock Solid Love/me • Beer Bottom/Scott McMenimen

14 – Rod Iron Residue/Cara Pinnick • Early Morning reminder/me

15 – Prickly Love in Sedona/Amy Mace Farnham

16 – The Grassy Knoll/me

17 – Gymrat Love/me • One Man's Trash/Noelle Federico Coppola • Watermark for Me/me

19 – Peekaboo/me

20 – What the Chip?/me • Streets of Love/me • Hello from here/me

21 – It's a Hard Love/me • Clay Finding/me

22 – For the Love of Vermont/Noelle Federico Coppola • Thank you Sheep/me

23 – Yesterdays Branch/JulieAnn McDougall

24 – Who Did That? :)/me

25 – Making the Guac/me • Deep in the Dirt/me • Sit Right Down/Noelle Federico Coppola

26 – Shaggy Love/me • Daily Reminder/me

27 – Stone Wall Heart/me • Afternoon Delight/me

28 – Dinner for the Bugs/me • Amongst the Others /me • Coconut YUM/me

29 – Signs of Love/me

30 – I Can Only Imagine/me

32 – Itty Bitty/me • Terazzo Wonder/me

33 – ChickyChickChick/Noelle Federico Coppola • At The Car Wash/me • Looking Right at Me/me

34 – Dangerous Love/me

35 – Warm & Cozy/me • What The WHAT?/me

36 – Standing Tall/me • Pickle, pickle, who has a pickle?/me • Upside Dinnertime/me

37 – Kitchen Smudge/me

38 – Concrete Romance/me • Messy Love/me

39 – In the River of Rocks/me • Simply Perfect/me • Strawberry Fields 4-eva/me

40 – Nestled on the Post/me

41 – Steppin on Up/me

42 – Baked to Perfection/Janet Burton • StreetSide likeness/me

43 – Queen Anne's Lace of love/me

44 – Down the Drain/me

45 – Step Step Stop/me • Happy for the Smudge/me

46 – Backyard LOVEs/me

48 – Bird in Love/me • Well Hello There/me • Love makes a way/me

49 – It's a Nutty kinda Love/me

50 – Massachusetts Memories/me

51 – Springtime Loveness/me • A feather in the kitchen!!?/me

52 – Weekend Lovings/me • Coffee dropped the love/me

53 – Lovers Bench/Noelle Federico Coppola • Amethyst Sparkle/me • Cracking me up/me

54 – With and Without/me

55 – Accidental Hole/me • Orange you Glad/me

56 – Asphalt Breakdown/Cara Pinnick • Stoop Step Stop/me • Squat Box Romance/me
57 – A Pile of Love from Luke/me
58 – Hand Me a Sprout/me • Seashells & more/Mindy Dutra
59 – Traveling Down a Path with Love/me
60 – Coffee Anyone?/me • Peppery Vinegar Romance/me
61 – Siftin' for Love/me
62 – Beneath MY Feet/me
63 – All Polished Up/me • Plantin some Love/me • Granite Surprise/Kathy Harkenrider
65 – Cast Iron in Love/me
66 – Love's Peeking Through/me
67 – Cheesy Love/me • DigItIn/me
68 – Melon Mess/me • Stoned Heart/me • Ziggy's Speckled Heart/Karysa Swackenberg & Luke McMenimen
69 – Painted Love/me
70 – Sidewalk View/me
71 – Amongst the Rubble/me • A Few of My Faves/me
72 – Look Again/me • Good Morning Darling/me
73 – LOVE Dipper/Abbey Rosher
74 – Rock of Somewhere/me • Simply Found Love/me • Snowy Days/Joy Tiernon
75 – Quadruplets in Love/me
76 – Alone in Love/me
78 – Stuck Between a Rock & a Hard Place/Joy Tiernon • I see you/Ali Dorman
79 – Cowhide Truth/me
80 – Love Me Hard/me • Monkey See/me • Little Lovely Finds/me
81 – Yoga Nights/me
82 – Elderberry Smudge/me • Weedy love/me
83 – Parsley's Got Passion/me
84 – Stopppp Right There/me
85 – Beauty Surrounds My Heart/me
86 – A Strong Proposition/me • Love is left Behind/me
87 – To & Fro - I see YOU/me
88 – Don't Trip on the Love/me
89 – Triplets in Love/me
90 – Love on the Line/me • Jetlagged Jetway/me • Slurpy Drop/me

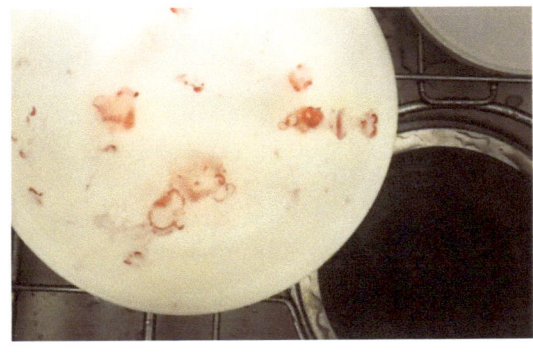  

91 – LOVE Cairn - Come Home/me
92 – My coffee Presssssin' Love/me
94 – Rockin it on the Carpet/me
95 – Outside In/me • Bootprints of Love/me
96 – Jesus Put That There/Sandy Bridges
97 – I'm Surrounded/me • A Hard Reminder/me • Love Spill/me
98 – Don't Step There/me • Healed Heart/Cara Pinnick
99 – I was Minding My Business/me
100 – After a Long Day/me
101 – The Spice of Love/me
102 – Tear Down the Wall/me
103 – Double Dose of Love/Melissa Little • Love in Walking/me
104 – A Hole in One/me • A Softer Love/me
105 – After the Rain/me • Ice Baby/me • Coffee Dropped It/me
106 – Just When I Needed It/me
107 – Beach Beauty/Mindy Dutra
108 – Down a Gravel Road/me • I've Fallen for Love/me
109 – Wholly Holey Love/me
110 – Heartgrain/me
111 – Is that Lovewood Forest?/JulieAnn McDougall • Stand Above the Crowd/me
112 – Well Hello There/me
113 – Rock Garden/Mary Reuse • David's Love Move/me
114 – Lovin Spoonfuls/me
115 – Scuff It Up/me • Everything but the kitchen sink/me • Tile Impasse to love/me
116 – Pot of Gold/me • Sending out an SOS/me
117 – Lean on Me/Allison Flesher
118 – Thanks Birdie/me • Dribble Drip Drop Heart/Francine Platt
119 – Hangin' Out with My Friends/me
120 – Precious Love/me
121 – Hardwood Softness/me • Coffee - Meet Marble/me • Love Magnified/me
123 – Marble - Meet Love/me
124 – Sonoran Quartz/Mark Briggs • Terazzo Mingle/me
125 – Mossy Romance/Dana Kelly
126 – XOXO/me • Crackin Me Up/me
127 – Living in the Shadows of Love/me
128 – Coffee Drop/Mindy Dutra • Loves Shadow/me • Look What I Found/me
129 – Watch Where You Walk/me
130 – Upside Down in a TN Restroom/me
131 – Birdie's Paradise/me • Standing Out in a Crowd/me
132 – My Morning Workout/me • Caught in the Middle/me • DripDripDrop/me
133 – Love in the Crosswalk/me • Watermark of Love/me
134 – Sweet Love/Renae Disney
135 – Sweetness/me • Messy Messy Love/me • Imprint in My Heart/me
136 – AUTHOR PIC: Steve Vordeman, Vorderman Photography

ABOUT THE AUTHOR

Tracy McMenimen

This first-time author, single mom, and beautiful daughter of the Most High King knows what it means to live in this fallen world. Having lived broken and bruised, it was discipline, perseverance and the power of the Holy Spirit that drove her to press on in the face of negativity, adversity and hardships. It was the love of family and friends that continued to pour into her that she is most grateful for.

She is passionate in her Christian walk and is driven to live from a place of joy, even in the madness and sadness of life. She is filled with God's love and continues to pour it out into the world, hence the creation of this book. She believes that it is LOVE that gets us through every day. Love of self. Love of God. Love for living. "Living on the God-side of life is a beautiful place to be," she says.

Tracy was brought up in a small town north of Boston with her two sisters. She has lived in Arizona, California, Idaho, and now resides in Indiana. She is a life coach, professional organizer, and local volunteer. In her free time she enjoys working in her yard, spending time with girlfriends, and basking in the sun. Aside from a lifestyle that includes a healthy diet and exercise, her hobbies include sewing memory quilts, as well as creating notecards, bookmarks, and vision boards.

Being engulfed with the love of God is what ignites her to keep going, giving, and loving.

www.ingramcontent.com/pod-product-compliance
Lightning Source LLC
Chambersburg PA
CBHW042055090526
44582CB00010B/163